Legacy-Driven Leadership
Volume 1: The Seeds of Legacy

By Jason Rogers

The Kimoja Initiative, LLC

Albany, New York 2025

Legacy-Driven Leadership: The Seeds of Legacy

© 2025 Jason Rogers. All rights reserved.

No part of this publication may be reproduced, stored in a retrieval system, or transmitted in any form or by any means: electronic, mechanical, photocopying, recording, or otherwise, without prior written permission from the author, except in the case of brief quotations used in reviews, articles, or educational settings with proper citation.

This book is a work of nonfiction. All names and examples are drawn from real-life leadership experiences or anonymized for illustrative purposes. Any resemblance to actual persons or institutions is purely coincidental unless noted.

Published by:
The Kimoja Initiative LLC
Albany, New York

www.thekimojainitiative.com
@the.kimoja.initiative

ISBN: 979-8-9997019-0-9
Library of Congress Control Number: 2025919954

Cover design, interior layout, and visual content created in partnership with The Kimoja Initiative and affiliated collaborators.

For professional inquiries or bulk licensing requests, please contact:

info@thekimojainitiative.com or visit
https://payhip.com/kimojainitiative

Visuals for each Legacy Seed were conceptualized by the author and brought to life through AI-assisted illustration tools, then refined to match the spirit and message of *Legacy-Driven Leadership*.

Foreword

My experience has taught me that leadership is never about titles, positions, or perfection. It's about presence. It's about relationships. Most importantly, it's about legacy. Legacy is defined by how others experience your leadership; what you nurture, how you show up, and the lasting impact you leave behind.

This book began as a collection of reflections and stories embedded in the weekly emails I sent to my faculty and staff as a first-time school leader in 2016. I understood that regular communication was necessary, but I felt an even deeper responsibility to root our work in something more: purpose, trust, and community.

In those weekly emails, I started with a quote or story and followed with a reflection to anchor our daily work in what matters most. I saved those emails over the three years I served in that building, not sure why at the time. As new roles and challenges came, I returned to them. They held up a mirror to my asks of others and my growth. They also became something else: legacy seeds.

I define legacy seeds as small, intentional choices rooted in reflection, care, and values. When nurtured, they grow into lasting transformation. Not overnight. But over time.

This first volume, *Legacy-Driven Leadership: The Seeds of Legacy*, gathers reflections from the earliest chapters of my leadership story. The content is organized around six foundational themes:

Vision, Trust, Presence, Accountability, Courage, and Purpose.

Each chapter offers multiple *Legacy Seeds*, along with visuals, captions, prompts, and space for growth. They invite you into ongoing dialogue with yourself and your leadership. Taken together, they can shape not just how you lead but how others grow because of your leadership. While this book is organized in a purposeful sequence, leadership growth is rarely linear. Each legacy seed stands on its own, so you can read cover to cover or turn to the reflection you need the most in that moment.

Whether you're preparing to step into your first leadership role or have been in this work for decades, I invite you to move slowly through these pages. Highlight. Pause. Revisit. Reflect.

Not everything will resonate at once, and that's okay. Legacy is a slow build. It requires humility, curiosity, and the courage to return to what you thought you already understood. You'll notice the concept of "performance" appearing often in these pages. That's because it captures the tension that every school leader faces: the pressure to perform versus the call to build something that lasts. Performance has its place, but it can't be the finish line. Legacy-driven leadership begins where performance ends.

Thank you for joining me on this journey. Let's grow forward together.

Jason Rogers
Co-Founder, The Kimoja Initiative

About the Author

Jason Rogers is a veteran educator, school leader, and leadership coach with nearly two decades of experience supporting students, teachers, and school leaders across New York State. He is the co-founder of The Kimoja Initiative LLC, a venture he leads alongside his wife, Tashawna. Together, they created Kimoja Educational Consulting and The Reset Within, two ventures under The Kimoja Initiative LLC umbrella that focus on school leadership development and personal transformation, respectively.

Jason brings both a deeply personal and professional lens to his work, rooted in his lived experience as a Black male educator navigating a field that has historically been shaped by inequity. As a Culturally Responsive Education (CRE) trainer, he has helped educators confront bias, reimagine practices, and center equity in classrooms and schools. His leadership in district and state-level equity initiatives has further underscored his commitment to creating spaces where belonging and justice are not aspirations, but expectations.

Throughout his career, Jason has served as a classroom

teacher, Assistant Principal, Principal, and state-level education leader for school improvement. In every role, he has remained anchored in one guiding belief: that transformative, legacy-driven leadership begins with trust, clarity of purpose, and the courage to reflect deeply.

This collection of visuals, quotes, and reflections is inspired by the weekly messages Jason shared with his faculty and staff during his first years as a school leader. These insights were sharpened through hallway conversations with staff and shaped in the quiet, intentional pauses that every leader must learn to embrace.

Whether you're a first-year teacher, a seasoned principal, or someone working behind the scenes to strengthen schools, this book invites you to reflect on your practice, recommit to your purpose, and honor the seeds of legacy you plant every day.

Table Of Contents

How to Use This Book: A Guide for Leaders Who Lead with Purpose 10

Reflective Journal Invitation 14

Facilitator's Guide Invitation 16

What Is Legacy-Driven Leadership? 18

Chapter One: Vision and Intention 20
    Legacy Seed: Tools and Intention 22
    Legacy Seed: Living in the Moment 29
    Legacy Seed: The Drum Circle (Leadership in Rhythm) 35
    Legacy Seed: Leaders Aren't Born, They're Guided 41
    Chapter One Closing Reflection: Catch the Vision 48

Chapter Two: Trust as the Foundation of Leadership 50
    Legacy Seed: The Cement of Trust 53
    Legacy Seed: Change Occurs at The Speed of Trust. 61
    Legacy Seed: You Can't Lead If You Don't Trust 67
    Legacy Seed: The Hidden Curriculum of Trust 72
    Chapter Two Closing Reflection: Trust Is the Thread That Holds It All Together 80

Chapter Three - The Presence Principle: Leading with Humanity at the Center 83
    Legacy Seed: Cultivate the Hum 85

Legacy Seed: Community Begins Where Authenticity Lives 90

Legacy Seed: The Importance of Building Relational Trust 97

Legacy Seed: Make Yourself Visible 103

Chapter Three Closing Reflection: The Presence Principle 110

Chapter Four: Growth and Accountability 112
Legacy Seed: Views From the Balcony 114

Legacy Seed: Students Rise When Adults Reflect ... 121

Legacy Seed: Leaders Shape What They Allow 127

Legacy Seed: Changing the World Starts with How We Lead 133

Legacy Seed: Before Goals, Feed Your Spirit 139

Legacy Seed: All Good Work Is Worthy of Dedication 146

Chapter Four Closing Reflection: Growth and Accountability 152

Chapter Five: Courage and Change 155
Legacy Seed: The Comfort Zone Is a Beautiful Place... 158

Legacy Seed: Aim for Success, Not Perfection 164

Legacy Seed: Change Takes Time 169

Legacy Seed: Strong Schools Aren't Loud, ... 175
They're Rooted 175

Chapter Five Closing Reflection: Courage and Change

....181

Chapter Six - Legacy and Purpose................ 184
Legacy Seed: Legacy Isn't Built Overnight 186

Legacy Seed: Success Isn't Built, It's Planted......... 190

Legacy Seed: A Cadre of Creatively Crazy Individuals Can Carry an Organization....................................... 195

Legacy Seed: You Can Either Be a Fountain or A Drain 201

Legacy Seed: The Greatest Gift is Your Presence ..206

Chapter Six Closing Reflection: Legacy & Purpose 211

Epilogue: The Seeds We Leave Behind............214

Closing Reflection: What a Seed Can Do......... 218

Acknowledgments 222

The Blueprint to Legacy-Driven Leadership ... 225

References and Recommended Reading....... 229

How to Use This Book: A Guide for Leaders Who Lead with Purpose

This book is designed to *meet you where you are.*

Whether you're stepping into leadership for the first time or have been leading for decades, *Legacy-Driven Leadership* is structured to support your growth, deepen your reflection, and amplify your impact.

Each chapter is organized by theme, <u>but the path you take through this book is yours to choose.</u>

There is no one "right" way to navigate this book, **only your way**. The design was both intentional and flexible. The chapters follow a natural progression, from vision to trust, presence, growth, courage, and legacy, so reading in order offers a purposeful journey. Yet leadership rarely unfolds in a straight line. Each legacy seed is also self-contained, so you can turn to the reflection you need most in the moment and still find meaning and practical guidance. Whether you read cover to cover or begin with the seed that speaks to where you are today, the goal is the same: to nurture your leadership and the legacy that you are planting.

Pause when you need to. Return to the seeds that resonate. Reflect in the margins. Grow at your pace.

And use the **Reflective Journal** and **Facilitator's Guide** to deepen your practice and extend the impact of your learning. Both are available for purchase.

You're not just reading a book.

It's a blueprint. A mindset. A legacy in motion.

What You'll Find in Each Chapter:

Each chapter includes a series of Legacy Seeds: visuals paired with narrative insights and opportunities for further insight.

You can:

- Move through the book from beginning to end for a comprehensive leadership journey.

- Or flip directly to a **Legacy Seed** that speaks to the moment you are in

Not Sure Where to Begin?

You decide how to navigate this book. Each legacy seed is its own rooted reflection, ready for you to visit when the season or moment calls for it.

- **Feeling stuck or overwhelmed?** Start with Chapter Five: Courage and Change.

- **Trying to build stronger relationships with your team?** Explore Chapter Two: Trust as the Foundation for Leadership.

- **Looking to reconnect with your deeper purpose?** Turn to Chapter Six: Legacy & Purpose.

Want to Go Deeper?

Each legacy seed also includes four sections designed to help you move from reflection to action:

- **Reflection Journal Starter** – a thought or question to spark your initial reflection and prepare your mindset. This serves as an entry point to your deeper work.

- **Reflection Prompt** – guiding questions that invite you to pause, think, write, and examine your own leadership practices from multiple angles.

- **Legacy Seed in Action** – a practical step you can take that encourages you to apply what you've been reflecting on to your daily leadership.

- **Legacy Checkpoint** – a moment to step back and connect what you've learned to the bigger picture of the legacy that you are cultivating.

The companion reflective journal and facilitator's guide offer prompts to help you deepen insights and bring them to life.

- **Reflective Journal** - A companion tool (available separately) for individual reflection and leadership action planning.

- **Facilitator's Guide** - Included as a digital download in the *Facilitator's Edition* of this book, perfect for group learning, PLCs, or leadership development teams.

Reflective Journal Invitation

Extend the Journey. Deepen the Roots.

Legacy-Driven Leadership: The Seeds of Legacy wasn't just written to be read; it was written to be reflected upon.

Each Legacy Seed in this volume is an invitation:

To slow down and examine your leadership.

To return to your values.

To lead with clarity, courage, and care.

But reflection doesn't happen automatically. It must be cultivated with time, space, and intention.

That's why the **Legacy-Driven Leadership Reflective Journal** was created. This companion resource (available as a separate purchase) is designed to help you dig deeper, stay grounded, and bring each Legacy Seed to life in your unique leadership context. It's designed to engage deeply with the legacy seeds and reflect intentionally on your leadership practice.

Inside the journal, you'll find:

- **Thought-provoking self-reflection prompts** aligned to each chapter.

- **Leadership Practice prompts** designed to push you to consider ways to apply your learning to your daily leadership practices.

- **Equity-lens prompts** that encourage you to interrogate your leadership skills through an equity and inclusion lens.

- **Room for pause**—because growth isn't just about what we do, but about who we become.

Whether you use this journal individually or alongside a leadership team, it's your space to **wrestle, wonder, and grow**. Legacy isn't built in a single moment; it's built through reflection, again and again.

Facilitator's Guide Invitation

Lead the Learning. Multiply the Impact.

The Legacy-Driven Leadership Facilitator's Guide is included as part of the *Facilitator's Guide Edition* of this book. It was created to support leadership coaches, professional development facilitators, school administrators, and equity-centered educators in designing meaningful, engaging learning experiences grounded in *The Seeds of Legacy* and the *Reflective Journal*.

This guide will transform the book's content into practical, purpose-driven sessions designed to deepen reflection and expand impact across teams, schools, or entire districts.

Each chapter of the guide includes:

- **Core themes and session objectives** aligned with the chapter's central leadership theme.

- **Facilitation flow** with framing strategies, suggested timing, and delivery tips.

- **Legacy Seed Exploration** with questions adapted from the reflective journal plus discussion extensions.

- **Equity Lens Prompts** that encourage participants to interrogate systems and power.

- **Legacy-in-Action Extensions** that ground each session in personal accountability.

- **High Engagement Activities** that facilitators can use or adapt in their work with participants.

Whether you're facilitating a 1:1 coaching conversation, a PLC session, or a full-day retreat, this guide helps translate reflective leadership into *real-world transformation*.

What Is Legacy-Driven Leadership?

Here's a definition drawn from the reflections, stories, and seeds explored throughout this book:

Legacy-driven leadership *is the intentional, equity-centered practice of leading with purpose, presence, and integrity to plant seeds of growth that outlast your tenure. Legacy-Driven Leadership is not defined by titles, checklists, or optics, but by the consistent way a leader shows up; for their people, their values, and their vision, especially when it's inconvenient or uncomfortable.*

Legacy-driven leaders:

- **Lead with vision** that is rooted in relationships, not just results.

- **Build trust** through consistent presence, follow-through, and cultural responsiveness.

- **Prioritize people over performance**, ensuring that every voice, especially those who are historically marginalized, is seen, heard, and valued.

- **Embrace discomfort** as a necessary condition

for growth and equity.

- **Hold themselves accountable first**, using reflection as both a leadership strategy and a moral compass.

- **Sow care, consistency, and courage** into the daily culture of their schools or organizations, knowing that leadership is lived in the small moments as much as the big ones.

Ultimately, legacy-driven leadership asks not, *"What did I accomplish?"* but *"What will endure because of how I led?"*

As you move through each chapter of this book, return to your evolving definition of *legacy-driven leadership*. Revisit it. Refine it. Let the reflections, stories, and strategies ahead challenge and deepen your understanding. Leadership grows, and so should your definition of the legacy you're building.

Chapter One: Vision and Intention

Visionary leadership doesn't happen by accident; it's cultivated. It's grounded in clarity, shaped by mentorship, refined through presence, and aligned in rhythm with the people we serve.

To lead with vision is more than setting direction. It's about staying rooted in purpose, even when the path forward is unclear. It's about tuning in, not just to plans, but to people. And it's about ensuring your "why" is felt, not just stated.

Tools can support the work, but tools alone don't build legacies; people do. Leaders who leave a lasting mark lead boldly, show up authentically in discomfort, and are guided first by purpose, intention, and values, not just short-term metrics and outcomes.

This chapter explores the dynamic relationship between vision and intention through four legacy seeds; each one offering a different lens on how leadership takes root and grows:

Legacy Seeds in This Chapter:

- **"Tools and Intention"** – *The why behind the tools matters more than the tools themselves.*

- **"Living in the Moment"** (Inspired by Thoreau) – *Presence is a leadership discipline, not a luxury.*

- **"The Drum Circle (Leadership in Rhythm)"** – *Culture has rhythm; leadership tunes it, not controls it.*

- **"Leaders Aren't Born; They're Guided"** *Mentorship shapes legacy; leadership is a shared becoming.*

With these seeds, we begin the journey of legacy-driven leadership, where vision is more than ambition, and intention is more than action. Together, they form the foundation for a leadership practice that lasts.

Legacy Seed: Tools and Intention

"Leadership isn't just about the tools. It's about the intention behind how those tools are used."

– Legacy-Driven Leadership.

Not Every Problem Is a Nail

In my early years as a school administrator, I believed that success depended on the size of my toolkit.

I had protocols for everything: discipline systems, data dives, PLCs, family engagement plans, the list can go on and on. With two Master's degrees and years of preparation, I felt ready for anything. I prided myself on being a "systems guy", someone who could diagnose an issue and apply the right protocol with precision and fidelity.

My ego told me that with the right tool and enough training, I could fix anything.

That mindset crystallized during my time as an assistant principal, hired with a clear mandate: address the rising suspension rates, especially among Black and Brown students. I knew the data. I knew the disproportionality. I had a plan.

One afternoon, a teacher came to me, visibly frustrated over a student. "He's checked out," she said. "I can't teach when he's constantly disrupting. We've tried everything."

She was talking about a student we had discussed before,

one whose name appeared often in discipline reports but rarely in student celebrations. I listened, nodded, and assured her I'd help.

That evening, I did what I had been trained to do. I analyzed his behavior data, cross-checked our intervention notes, and prepared my plan. I scheduled a follow-up meeting and arrived with a folder in hand, ready to provide solutions.

"We're drawing a line in the sand," I said confidently.

What I didn't realize in that moment was that I wasn't solving a problem. I was reinforcing a pattern. I was prioritizing the wrong thing. My intent was to support the needs of the teacher. In trying to ease her frustration, I validated a cycle that had created the very disparities I was tasked with dismantling.

I hadn't asked if the student had been spoken to. I hadn't looked at whether Tier 1 supports were being *implemented* in that classroom and whether they were *implemented with fidelity*. I didn't ask whether that student felt connected to even one adult in the building. Fifteen minutes into the conversation, realization hit: I had walked in with a hammer, assuming the problem was a nail. I pivoted.

I had chosen action over reflection. Control over curiosity.

That wasn't leadership. That was ego disguised as expertise.

What the teacher needed wasn't another plan. She needed a thought partner; someone to help her reframe, reflect, and rediscover a sense of possibility. What the student needed wasn't removal. He needed a connection. Presence. Someone willing to ask, "What's going on beneath the surface of the data and intervention notes?" That moment reshaped how I approached leadership. Not every problem is a nail, and leadership isn't about swinging harder. It's about knowing when to put the hammer down.

Tools Don't Build Legacy—Intention Does

It's tempting to lead like a builder, measuring success by how many problems we solve or systems we implement. But schools aren't construction sites, and people aren't projects. Leadership isn't just about efficiency. It's about *discernment*.

True leadership asks:

Is this a moment for action, or a moment for listening?

Am I reaching for this tool because it's what the situation requires or because it's what I've always used?

Is this solution aligned with my values or simply convenient?

When leaders treat every challenge like a nail, the hammer becomes the default tool. Coaching turns into compliance. Conversations turn directive. Innovation stalls. Trust erodes. And the most well-intentioned initiatives feel like burdens instead of movements.

But when you lead with intention, your tools become more than instruments; they become invitations. As Leithwood and colleagues (2023) remind us, leadership is second only to teaching in its impact on student learning. The hammer matters, but it's the vision and skill of the carpenter that determine what gets built.

You lead with intention by listening. By co-creating solutions. By giving your team permission to think, to feel, to challenge, to grow.

Stop asking only *"What are we building?"* and start asking, *"Who is it for?"* and *"Who are we becoming as we build it?"*

That's when strategy aligns with humanity. That's when tools serve people, not the other way around. That's when leadership becomes legacy.

Reflection Journal Starter

Legacy isn't defined by how many tools we carry. It's defined by how intentionally we use them. As a leader, your intention speaks louder than any checklist or protocol. It's not just what you reach for; it's why, when, and with whom.

Reflection Prompt:

Think back to a moment when you reached for a tool or strategy without taking a moment to pause and reflect.

What was your intention in that moment? How did it impact the people who were involved? What might have shifted if you had taken a moment to pause and reflect before reaching for that tool?

Legacy Seed in Action:

Before using your next leadership tool, ask two colleagues how that tool could best support shared goals. Make any adjustments based on that feedback and explain why those changes were made. Tools only carry weight when they're rooted in intention, and modeling this process shows your team that it's not the tool itself that matters, but the purpose and the people that the tool serves.

Legacy Checkpoint:

Legacy-driven leadership that lasts doesn't begin with a toolkit. It begins with clarity of purpose. The tools you use will change, but your intention behind your choice of the tool is what shapes the culture.

Your leadership legacy isn't built by how many "hammers" you carry but by the wisdom you use to know *when* and *when not to* use one.

When you lead with intention and discernment, the work becomes collaborative, not corrective. Your tools become *instruments of empowerment*, not enforcement. And the culture you shape isn't just well-run; it's deeply rooted in purpose and intention.

Legacy Seed: Living in the Moment

"You must live in the present, launch yourself on every wave, find your eternity in each moment. Fools stand on their island of opportunities and look toward another land. There is no other land; there is no other life but this."

— Henry David Thoreau.

Living in the Moment

It's easy to believe the myth that urgency equals excellence...especially in our profession. From the moment you walk into the building, there's pressure to move fast, react instantly, and respond constantly. Emails, walk-throughs, staff needs, phone calls, and student crises have become your driving factors before lunch.

If you're not careful, leadership becomes reactive rather than responsive, a constant chase instead of a grounded presence. You become a firefighter, extinguishing flare-ups without fully addressing the faulty wiring that caused the fire. Over time, everything starts to feel like an emergency, and moments of calm feel unfamiliar or even unearned.

But presence, *true* presence, isn't about how many tasks you complete. It's about how fully you engage with what and who is in front of you. A sense of urgency without clarity will lead to burnout; for you and for those that you lead.

Thoreau's quote is about interrupting our habit of deferral: understanding that life isn't a 'waiting room' for something better, and leadership isn't a sprint toward a calmer, clearer future. There is no "next land" where everything settles. This moment...this hallway conversation, this team meeting, this classroom visit- is the only one you're guaranteed. And how you show up in it matters.

Operating at 80% while being emotionally depleted, mentally distracted, and physically tense isn't sustainable. You may get the work done, but the absence of your full self will be felt. Staff sense when you're rushed. Students notice when your eyes flick to your phone. The school community absorbs the energy of your leadership. When that energy is strained, it echoes throughout the building. As the saying goes, you can't pour from an empty cup.

The solution isn't more hustle, it's more *humanity*.

Reclaim your Time

To lead well, you must reclaim time to reflect. Build margin into your day, not as a luxury, but as a necessity. That means scheduling a protected window of time each day where you are not in a reactive mode. It means trusting others with what you don't need to hold onto alone. When you hold everything, you lose the ability to hold anything in depth. By empowering others to lead in their lane, you create space to lead with intention in yours.

Leadership isn't just about what you do for others. It's about how you care for yourself so you can serve with clarity and compassion. Let a trusted colleague hold you accountable for the time that you protect. Delegate meaningfully and with intention; not to offload the work, but to uplift potential.

Reclaim the moment. Before you open your inbox, take a quiet walk through the building. Sit with a teacher in their classroom just to listen. Stand in the hallway, without a clipboard or computer, and simply tune into the hum of the community that you're cultivating.

Presence is a radical act of leadership in a world addicted to speed. Let yourself be here.

This is the wave.

This is the moment.

Launch yourself.

When you return to the work rested, clear, grounded, you'll lead not from depletion, but from wholeness. And from that wholeness, your people will feel the difference. When a leader is present, the culture breathes easier. Rather than being a firefighter, you become a gardener, cultivating growth with patience, and pruning what no longer serves while planting seeds that will bloom with time.

Reflection Journal Starter

In a role often defined by urgency, it's easy for school leaders to race through the day, checking boxes, putting out fires, and mistaking motion for progress. But presence isn't a luxury in leadership; it's a *discipline.*

Living in the moment means *knowing when to pause, when to listen, and when to center people over tasks.* The moments in which you're most present often reveal your core values. The moments you disconnect may reveal where those values are being stretched too thin.

Reflection Prompt:

What adjustments can you make today - whether in your schedule, in your mindset, or through delegation practices - to shift away from a state of hyper-vigilance and into a state of responsive leadership?

Legacy Seed in Action:

Block a ten-minute non-negotiable slot of time tomorrow. Use this time to walk through your building without an agenda and engage with three people.

Legacy Checkpoint:

Legacy isn't just shaped by big decisions; it's shaped in the quiet moments of care, reflection, and presence.

By living in the moment, you model a kind of leadership that is sustainable, relational, and deeply human. And in doing so, you plant seeds of legacy that will outlast any meeting agenda.

Fires may draw attention, but gardens sustain life. Legacy-driven leadership means leading like a gardener; planting, pruning, and preparing for harvest.

Legacy Seed: The Drum Circle (Leadership in Rhythm)

"Destiny has a rhythm. You must surround yourself with people who have the same rhythm. Otherwise, they threaten to kill your creativity, and you will most certainly kill theirs."

— *Michael Arterberry.*

The Rhythm of School

Don't confuse *noise for rhythm.*

Every school has a sound. Sometimes it's a steady collective rhythm that carries an entire school community forward. Other times, it's just noise; scattered motion without alignment or intention.

You can hear it in hallway conversations, in the tone of staff meetings, in the energy of classrooms, or even in the silence of disengaged staff members. It can tell you whether trust is present, whether clarity exists, and whether systems and school community values are working in harmony.

There are moments when everything flows, and the rhythm is steady and collective. Teachers collaborate naturally. Grade-level teams operate in cohesion. Norms are honored. Students know what to expect.

At other times, the rhythm feels scattered and uneven. One classroom pulses with joy, rigor, and curiosity, while another sits in quiet frustration. One team hums with energy while another is fragmented. Even when academic outcomes look steady on the surface, the underlying beats matter. The rhythm of a school shapes how people feel when they enter a building and how they feel when they leave.

As a school leader, your role is not to force the rhythm; it's to tune it. You cannot command rhythm into place. It must be listened to, felt, nurtured, and adjusted. Rhythm should be present even when you're absent; not transform into noise. Just as a music producer sits at a soundboard before making adjustments, leadership begins with observation. What's working? Where is the energy flowing? Where is it blocked? These aren't questions rooted in blame. They're rooted in a quest for alignment.

You might discover a team thriving in collaboration while another operates in silos. One grade-level team may have clear instructional norms while another seems unsure of what a shared practice even means. In some classrooms, innovation flourishes. In others, teachers wait silently for permission to innovate. These mismatches create dissonance, not just in routines, but in trust itself; even small misalignments can weaken confidence in the leader and the team. And over time, people adjust their rhythms according to their level of comfort to compensate. Some speed up to cover gaps. Some slow down to avoid burnout. Some may check out entirely. Slowly, the unified beat fades, and what once moved in harmony becomes unrecognizable noise.

It's important to keep in mind that rhythm isn't about speed. It's not about how fast you move. It's about how well you move together. Leadership in rhythm is about presence, clarity, and the willingness to pause when needed. Sometimes that means cancelling a rollout to focus on restoring foundational norms and systems. Sometimes it means creating authentic spaces for teachers to use their voice; not just for collecting feedback, but for acting on it.

Rhythm can be rebuilt in the smallest moment. One conversation that resets expectations. One check-in with a teacher to reaffirm connections. One celebration that reminds people that they're seen. You won't bring the entire school community back into sync overnight, but you can begin by listening more than reacting, aligning more than assigning, and moving with (and not ahead of) your stakeholders.

In a true drum circle, no one leads by playing over others. The leader listens for the subtle cues. They hear where things are misaligned and gently guide the group back together. Leadership is not about volume; it's about connection. It's about tuning in so that the culture can breathe again.

Let the beat build.

Reflection Journal Starter:

Leadership is more than coordination; it's **calibration**.

Every school has a rhythm: a pulse shaped by its people, systems, and guiding values. Some rhythms are harmonious; others are disjointed. As a leader, your role isn't to force **uniformity**; it's to foster **alignment**: a collective rhythm where each voice, each beat, and each contribution is honored.

When you attune yourself to the cadence of your school, the subtle rhythms of classrooms, daily conversations, and interactions, you begin to hear what is strong, where there are disconnects, and where deeper alignment is needed.

Reflection Prompt:

What is your school's current rhythm revealing? How might you tune your leadership to honor alignment without silencing individual voices?

Legacy Seed in Action:

Attend one team meeting this week as a silent observer. Resist the urge to steer the conversation. Instead, listen for the rhythm of the group, where their voices align and where there are moments where they fall out of sync. Afterwards, share one example of intentional alignment that you witnessed and affirm how it moved the team forward.

Legacy Checkpoint:

In schools, **rhythm is culture made visible**.

A leader's legacy isn't found in the noise they make, but in their ability to listen deeply, align meaningfully, and restore collective movement. When leaders guide in rhythm, they don't just manage systems; they sustain communities. And when aligned, those communities move forward together.

Don't mistake noise for rhythm. Leadership that honors rhythm builds a legacy that lasts.

Legacy Seed: Leaders Aren't Born, They're Guided

"No one is born a leader. You become one through experience, learning, and the influence of others."

— *Unknown.*

Debunking the Myth

The myth of the "natural-born leader" is both seductive and dangerous. It suggests that some people are wired to lead; arriving in this world equipped with charisma, confidence, and clarity, ready to inspire, influence, and command. But leadership isn't a birthright. It's a responsibility, and one that is earned, not inherited.

Those who've worn the weight of the principalship or stood before a team in uncertain times know the truth: leadership is forged, not gifted. It's shaped in the crucible of experience, through hesitation, through vulnerability, through failure, and course correction. Behind every seasoned leader is a path lined with missteps, moments of doubt, and the slow, courageous work of becoming.

Many of us remember the first time we were seen before we were ready. A supervisor invited us into a space we hadn't yet led. A mentor gave honest feedback that stung, but stuck. A colleague asked the hard questions that made us better, not just more comfortable. These moments didn't happen by accident. They were intentional. They were evidence of someone choosing to guide rather than manage. To invest rather than gatekeep. And that choice changed everything.

The Power of Mentorship

The best school leaders never forget how they were shaped through experiences that someone created for them. It wasn't just chance that brought them to the table; it was someone offering them the mic before they had mastered the message. Someone who didn't wait for them to prove they were ready, but trusted that they could grow into readiness.

That's the kind of leadership we need now: leaders who deliberately build pathways for others. Not just by assigning tasks, but by offering real opportunities; inviting aspiring voices to lead parts of meetings, to co-facilitate PDs, or to shadow decision-making processes. These aren't symbolic gestures. These opportunities are growth labs, and every school needs more of them.

Equally important is how we talk to those we're developing. Flattery doesn't build leaders; feedback does. Honest, specific, and consistent feedback helps educators move from potential to practice. If you're not offering feedback that makes people pause and reflect, you may be offering comfort instead of growth.

As a leader, this means carving out space, not just to evaluate, but to coach. Make it a regular rhythm; schedule quarterly development check-ins with those you see rising. Ask: *What are you learning? Where do you want to grow? How can I support your next step?* The time you invest in these conversations will pay dividends in the culture and sustainability of your school.

Leadership as Stewardship

Leadership development is a sacred responsibility. If our goal is to build sustainable, student-centered systems, we must approach adult development with the same urgency and intentionality we bring to student achievement.

That means leading transparently. Talk about your growth. Let your team hear the questions you're wrestling with, the mistakes you've made, and the learning you're still doing. This models a culture where growth is the goal, not perfection. And it gives permission for others to show up as learners, too.

We also need to shift our mindset from leadership as authority to leadership as accountability. Authority says, "I have the title, so follow me." Accountability says, "I'll model the work, and we'll grow together." It's not about being the smartest voice in the room; it's about building a room where everyone can lead. That means you can't guard your title or position like a gatekeeper, a mistake that we often make as leaders. Gatekeeping blocks growth, erodes trust, and leaves your school dependent on one person. It means finding joy in the daily work of being humbled; of learning, listening, and remembering that leadership is never about you alone. If your leadership ends with you, it was never legacy; it was ego.

Humility is not a weakness or loss of authority; it's often where the deepest joy of leadership is found. Humility creates space for growth, connection, and shared purpose. The joy comes when leaders realize that their role isn't to be above those they serve, but to be with them, lifting, learning, and leaving something greater behind.

To Those Still Becoming

For those still finding their way, new teachers, aspiring deans, assistant principals just beginning to see what's possible, know this: you are not behind. You are becoming. The discomfort you feel isn't a flaw. It's evidence that you are stretching. And that stretch is part of the journey all great leaders take.

True leadership is less about control and more about care. Less about certainty and more about learning. And it never happens alone. When someone invites you in, offers honest feedback, or challenges you with love, accept it. That is legacy in motion.

...and if you're able to offer that to someone else? Do it. Name their potential. Offer opportunities before they ask. Create spaces for them to practice while learning. Leadership is not something we arrive at; it's something we pass on.

Someone once made space for you. Now it's your turn to do the same.

Reflection Journal Starter

Leadership is not an individual pursuit; it's a continuum that's shaped by guidance, challenge, and care. None of us arrives in a position of leadership fully formed. The most impactful school leaders are those who remember the mentors who selflessly poured themselves into them and subsequently choose to pay that forward.

Leadership-driven legacy isn't defined by how far a school leader goes, but by how many people they bring with them.

Reflection Prompt:

Who are you intentionally guiding? How will your leadership ripple through the leaders you develop?

Legacy Seed in Action:

Invite an emerging leader to co-facilitate a portion of an upcoming meeting. Meet with them beforehand, clarifying the purpose of the meeting, structure, and expected outcomes. Afterwards, take the time to debrief together: highlight what worked well and offer growth-oriented suggestions. Guiding new leaders this way multiplies your impact; every time you share leadership, you plant seeds.

Legacy Checkpoint:

True leadership is generational. Your legacy isn't in the policies you wrote or the meetings you led. It's in the people you developed and in the humility you showed along the way. Great leaders aren't remembered for being the smartest in the room. They're remembered for how they lifted others. Reflect often to ensure that you're leading in a way that creates a pipeline for others, not a bottleneck that blocks them.

Chapter One Closing Reflection: Catch the Vision

-Legacy-Driven Leadership

"Once vision is clear, trust is the first condition for execution. It establishes the culture and relationships needed to move any vision forward."

– Legacy-Driven Leadership.

Vision isn't a poster on the wall; it's a posture. It's a way of showing up each day with clarity, consistency, and purpose. Legacy-driven leadership begins here, not in ambition alone, but in intention.

In this chapter, you were reminded that tools alone don't make a leader or drive impact; intention does. Leadership rooted in purpose outlasts any checklist. *(Tools and Intention)*

You embraced the discipline of presence, knowing that clarity and calm aren't luxuries; they're leadership essentials. *(Living in the Moment)*

You tuned your leadership to the culture's rhythm, learning that alignment, not control, is what sustains collective movement. *(The Drum Circle)*

You reflected on the truth that leaders aren't born, they're developed. Legacy is shaped through mentorship, guidance, and shared growth. *(Leaders Aren't Born, They're Guided)*

Each of these seeds points to a deeper truth: Purpose without people is incomplete.

Chapter Two: Trust as the Foundation of Leadership

Even the clearest vision will stall without one essential force beneath it, **trust.**

Trust isn't a bonus in leadership; it's the foundation.

It's the cement that binds vision to action. The bridge that spans fear and uncertainty. And the silent force that determines how far, and how fast, a school can grow.

Without trust, even the most promising plans collapse under the weight of doubt. Communication becomes noise. Innovation stalls. Culture fractures.

This chapter examines how school leaders build, sustain, and model trust at every level of their practice. From staff meetings to student interactions, from hallway conversations to hard decisions, trust is cultivated in how we show up, how we follow through, and how we make others feel.

Trust isn't built by accident; it's built through intention. Through patterns. Through presence. And in a time when school communities are navigating change, challenge, and complexity, trust becomes the most important tool a leader can carry.

In the seeds that follow, we explore how:

Trust holds a school's communication together.

Trust determines the speed of change.

Trust must be mutual and modeled first by leadership.

Trust shapes what students feel, even when it's never named aloud.

Trust isn't just a leadership strategy; it's the soil. Everything else grows from there.

Legacy Seeds in This Chapter:

- **"The Cement of Trust"** – *Communication is only as strong as the trust that carries it. Trust is the foundation.*

- **"Change Occurs at the Speed of Trust"** – *Strategies can't outrun a deficit of trust.*

- **"You Can't Lead If You Don't Trust"** – *Trust is reciprocal and must be modeled.*

- **"The Hidden Curriculum of Trust"** – *Trust is the soil where student safety grows.*

Legacy Seed: The Cement of Trust

"Effective communication is built on the cement of trust, and trust is built on trustworthiness, not politics."

– *Legacy-Driven Leadership.*

Where Vision Meets Credibility

There's a quiet moment every school leader encounters...just before a tough conversation, just after a staff meeting that didn't land, or in the stillness of a hallway between classroom observations. In that moment, a question lingers:

Will they trust what I have to say?

In leadership, communication isn't just about clarity. It's about credibility.

You can deliver a message that's perfectly aligned with your goals, articulate, urgent, even inspiring, but if trust hasn't been built, it will echo instead of connecting. It may be heard, but it won't move people. In schools, people don't follow a strategy alone; they follow a belief. And belief is built through trust.

It's rarely about what is said.

It's about what people believe when they hear it.

A Lesson in Leadership

I learned this lesson early in my leadership journey.

Minutes after leading a back-to-school professional development session as a new principal, a group of teachers approached me. Their words were blunt: "We don't trust you."

We had just met. I hadn't expected that level of directness, and I wasn't prepared for it.

But in that moment, I realized their response wasn't really about me. It was about what came before me: broken promises, inconsistent leadership, and patterns of being dismissed. I had stepped into a space already shaped by fractured trust.

Instead of reacting defensively, I responded with calm and clarity. I told them I didn't expect their trust automatically. I intended to earn it through consistent action, not just words. And I acknowledged that trust was already in deficit, long before I arrived.

That moment shaped everything that came after. It taught me this simple truth:

Leadership doesn't start with vision. It starts with credibility. Credibility is impossible without trust.

Trust Is the Cement

If leadership is a bridge, designed to carry your intentions, expectations, and values from one side to your team on the other, then trust is the cement that holds it all together.

You can have clear plans, solid policies, and polished talking points. But without trust to bind those elements, the structure falters. The weight of your leadership won't hold. The message may be sound, but the delivery system is fragile.

Trust is what strengthens the connections between your message and your people. It reinforces every component: your tone, your presence, your follow-through.

It doesn't get poured in all at once. It's laid in small, intentional layers. You build it when your actions align with your words. You reinforce it when you follow through without needing to follow up. You strengthen it when hard conversations are met with honesty, not spin. You protect it when your listening is real—not just rehearsed.

Even silence sends a message.

When hallway concerns go ignored or meaningful

feedback is delayed, your inaction becomes part of your communication. Every email, every meeting, every interaction - they don't just share information, they signal what you value.

Those signals either bind the bridge tighter or let the structure weaken.

Trust as Structure, Not Softness

Effective school leaders understand trust isn't a soft skill; it's a structural one.

It gives your leadership form and strength. It allows your words to carry weight and your expectations to feel grounded rather than imposed. It enables your team to interpret your decisions through a lens of belief, not suspicion.

In schools, that belief matters. Without trust, change is fragile. With trust, change becomes sustainable, even when it's uncomfortable. Research shows that when trust is high, teachers are more likely to collaborate and persist through change (Hong, 2020; Bukko, 2021). Trust isn't a detour; it's the main road forward.

If you want to communicate with impact, focus less on saying it right and more on being someone worth listening to.

That means beginning staff meetings with transparency, not just agenda points. It means taking hallway feedback seriously and responding with presence. It means making space for your team to offer feedback through conversations that matter.

It means remembering this: trust isn't built in big speeches. It's built in how you show up on regular days, in ordinary moments, with extraordinary consistency.

The Weight of Your Words

Pause and ask yourself:

When you speak, are your words being carried by trust or collapsing under the weight of uncertainty?

Is your team interpreting your leadership through a foundation of credibility, or are they still navigating past fractures?

When trust is the cement, your leadership becomes more than communication. It becomes a connection. It becomes alignment. It becomes a relationship.

Relationships built on trust are strong enough to carry

your leadership forward, across the tough moments, through the stretch of change, and into the legacy you leave behind.

Reflection Journal Starter:

Trust isn't built in grand gestures; it's cemented in small, consistent acts. It's in the way we respond when tension rises, in the tone we use when people are unsure, in how we hold space, follow through, and show up again and again, especially when it's hard. As a school leader, your communication isn't just about information; it's about affirmation. Your presence isn't just seen, it's felt. When trust is strong, your team moves with confidence. When it's weak, everything wobbles.

Reflection Prompt

How are your daily habits and communication patterns either cementing or cracking the foundation of trust with your staff...especially across lines of identity, power, and experience?

Legacy Seed in Action:

Open your next meeting by highlighting a faculty or staff member who followed through on a commitment. Specifically name the commitment and connect it to trust and how it's reinforced with the team. Trust is built in moments like these – where promises and commitments are kept.

Legacy Checkpoint:

Strong leaders aren't just good communicators. They're **trusted** ones. The legacy of your leadership won't be measured solely by the plans you introduce; it will be measured by the **trust you build**. It won't be defined by whether your staff agrees with your decisions, but whether they trust the **intention** behind them. Trust is the bridge. But consistency is the cement.

Lay each brick with intention.

Because your empathy, presence, and follow-through don't just support your leadership; they **define it**.

Lay each brick with care.

Trust is what holds the whole house up.

Legacy Seed: Change Occurs at The Speed of Trust

"Change occurs at the speed of trust. Build the relationship, and the momentum will follow."

— Stephen Covey.

Change is inevitable, but transformation is optional. And the difference between the two often hinges on a single word: trust.

As a leader, you can build the most innovative plan. Design a masterful schedule. Craft a compelling vision for instructional reform. But if your team doesn't believe in you or each other, that change will stall and won't take root. The change may be announced and documented. It may even be posted on the professional development calendar. But it won't live in classrooms. It won't shift mindsets. It won't reshape the culture. It won't last.

Schools Aren't Machines - They're Ecosystems

The change won't last because schools aren't machines. They're ecosystems; dynamic, human, relational. Rooted in relationships. Trust is the oxygen that allows those systems to breathe, grow, and adapt.

Change fails not because educators are resistant. Most often, it fails because educators are wise. They know that every new initiative requires vulnerability:

To try.

To fail.

To grow in public.

And they'll only take that risk if they feel safe. Not just physically, but also *psychologically safe*. They need to know that their attempts won't be met with shame, silence, or blame. That kind of safety doesn't come from compliance, fidelity checklists, or mandates. It comes from trust.

Trust that their voices shaped the process.

Trust that the "why" behind the shift is clear, student-centered, and rooted in shared values.

Trust that if something doesn't go as planned, the response will be support, not punishment.

Leading For Trust, Not Just Change

As a school leader, your job isn't just to push change forward. It's to prepare the conditions that allow change to move forward. That preparation isn't laid with pressure; neither is it started with a memo. It begins with presence.

You build trust when you show up in real conversations, not just staff meetings. You build it when you pause rollout plans to gather genuine feedback and then adjust them based on what you hear. You build it when you admit what you don't know and model a posture of learning alongside your team.

With this type of leadership, decisions move not just with urgency, but with care. Strategy is tethered to values. The change you seek resonates with the heart of the school community, not just the needs of the system.

When Change Stalls, Start with Trust

If change is stalling, resist the urge to tighten the screws. Instead, loosen the screws and revisit your trust-building practices.

Ask yourself:

Who among your staff, students, or families might be waiting to feel seen, safe, or supported before they're ready to buy into changes in practices, procedures, or policy?

Have I moved too fast for people to catch their breath or voice their concerns?

Trust isn't a detour on the road to transformation. It is the road. And sometimes, *to go fast, you have to go slow.*

Reflection Journal Starter

Change isn't just about **strategy**; it's about trust. When people trust the *why* behind your decisions, and they believe in you, they'll walk with you through uncertainty. But when trust is thin, even the most thoughtful plans can collapse under the weight of doubt.

How you introduce change signals whether it's something done *to* your team or *with* them. Trust is built not in the rollout, but in the relationships that precede the rollout.

Listen deeply.

Invite challenge without defensiveness.

Center voices that are often left out of the room.

These aren't just soft skills. They're legacy-driven moves. They're how transformation begins to take root...one conversation at a time.

Reflection Prompt:

When leading change, how are you building trust, not just in the vision, but in the people you're asking to carry it forward?

Legacy Seed in Action:

Before introducing a new initiative, hold a 15-minute listening session with staff to capture their top concerns. Open the listening session with one guiding question, and then listen without defending or persuading. Document what is said and make adjustments (if needed) to the new initiative. Trust will not come from the new initiative itself. It will come from how school leaders engage with the people who are asked to carry it forward.

Legacy Checkpoint

Trust is not a detour on the path to change; it's the foundation that holds the weight of it. When you slow down to build trust, you don't lose momentum; you create it. Legacy-driven leaders don't just implement plans; they earn belief. That belief is what carries change forward... long after the rollout ends.

Legacy Seed: You Can't Lead If You Don't Trust

"You can't lead people if you don't trust them - and they won't follow you if they don't trust you."

- John Maxwell.

You Can't Lead If You Don't Trust

There's a common refrain in leadership circles: *"You have to earn trust."* And while there's truth in that, it's only half the story. Leadership begins not with being trusted, but with trusting others.

You can't lead if **you** don't trust.

Trust isn't a badge you earn after years in a role. It's a mindset, a daily choice to believe in the people you've hired, developed, and asked to show up for students. It's the quiet courage to let go, even when it feels easier to grip tighter. It's what transforms hierarchy into partnership, and what turns management into legacy.

Every school has a culture; whether high-performing or struggling, that culture rides on a current. Trust is either the undercurrent that carries the school forward or the force that quietly pulls it apart.

This current isn't shaped by grand decisions alone. It's defined in the small, everyday interactions. When a teacher voices a concern, does your response reflect curiosity or defensiveness? When mistakes happen, does your team brace for impact or feel safe to learn and grow? These moments reveal more about your leadership than any title ever could.

It's in these seemingly ordinary moments that trust is either built or broken.

And when it's broken or never extended, compliance becomes the substitute. Staff show up to meetings, but their presence is guarded. They nod during rollouts but disengage when implementation begins. They follow protocol but hold back passion. Often, it's not the change itself they resist; it's the lack of trust in the person leading it.

But when trust is present, something shifts. Teachers speak up without fear of judgment. They take instructional risks because they know growth is celebrated, not penalized. Teams collaborate from a sense of shared investment instead of obligation.

That shift begins with the leader.

It begins when you respond to concerns with listening, not just politeness, but genuine presence. When you share decisions rooted in your core values, even when the outcome is unpopular. When you acknowledge what you don't know and invite your team into the problem-solving process.

And it continues when you stop hoarding decisions out of fear. Leadership isn't weakened by distributing responsibility; it's strengthened. *Trusting teachers to adapt curriculum, encouraging emerging leaders to challenge outdated practices, and giving teams the autonomy to find their rhythm; these aren't signs of passivity. They are signs of belief.*

Belief in your people. Belief in their capacity. The belief that shared ownership leads to deeper commitment.

It's not about stepping back; it's about standing with. Trust, when extended first, comes back multiplied. And as it grows, so does the health of your culture. Fear recedes. Courage rises. And a spirit of collaboration becomes the norm, not the exception.

So, if you're wondering where to begin, start by asking yourself, "Have I shown them that I trust them?"

Because leadership rooted in trust creates the very conditions in which legacy can take root.

Reflection Journal Starter

Trust is not only something you build, it's something you extend. This legacy seed reminds us that leadership rooted in trust doesn't just feel good; it creates the conditions for others to thrive. When people feel genuinely trusted, they show up with more creativity, courage, and commitment. But when trust is withheld—intentionally or unconsciously—it signals doubt, breeds fear, and diminishes potential.

Legacy-driven leadership asks us to examine not just how much we are trusted, but how much trust we give and to whom.

Reflection Prompt:

Are you building a culture where all team members feel genuinely trusted by you? If not, what assumptions, habits, or biases might be getting in the way?

Legacy Seed in Action:

Delegate a meaningful decision to your team this week and resist the urge to override their choice. Afterwards, intentionally affirm their decision publicly to reinforce trust.

Legacy Checkpoint

Leadership without trust is noise without meaning. The true measure of your leadership is not found in compliance; it's found in the culture you cultivate. When trust is the foundation, leadership becomes relational, not positional.

Legacy Seed: The Hidden Curriculum of Trust

"When a teacher demonstrates sincerity and decisiveness in the classroom, the children will unconsciously give him or her permission to teach them…and without that permission, learning won't happen."

- Dr. Lorraine Monroe.

There's a quiet test every classroom must pass...one that doesn't show up in lesson plans or walkthrough rubrics:

Is this a space where students feel that they can exhale?

In the opening weeks of each school year, I would pose this exact question to my staff, not as a rhetorical challenge, but as a call for honest reflection. Behind every pencil, backpack, and raised hand is a student carrying something unseen. Peggy McIntosh refers to it as "The Invisible Knapsack" (1988). A student's invisible knapsack is filled with everything that they mentally carry with them daily. For many students, that knapsack is filled not with privilege, but with:

Uncertainty

Guardedness

Survival-mode thinking

That knapsack doesn't automatically get dropped just because the student walks into a school building or a classroom. It gets dropped when students *feel* a level of safety.

Safety Is Not Compliance

Safety is not built through control, and trust isn't created by charm or charisma. Students don't learn from adults simply because they're in charge. They learn from adults they believe. From adults who are consistent, fair, and authentic. From adults who demonstrate both **sincerity** *(the emotional honesty that makes them relatable)* and **decisiveness** *(the clarity that makes them dependable).*

Trust begins when students sense that their presence won't be punished, and their needs won't be minimized. *That starts with how teachers are led.*

Culture Starts Before the Bell

This work doesn't live solely within the four walls of a classroom. The conditions that allow a student to exhale are cultivated long before the morning bell rings. Safe classrooms don't appear by accident. They're the reflection of a broader climate, and that climate is shaped, in large part, by how school leaders show up.

A school leader who prioritizes presence over optics will foster a school where safety is practiced, not just promised. That means slowing down long enough to listen for tension in the hallway, asking deeper questions during check-ins, and modeling transparency in team meetings, especially when plans shift.

It means embedding safety into the system itself; rethinking observation cycles to feel like coaching and carving out protected spaces where staff can be candid without fear of consequence. If we want all students to feel seen, we must first ensure that all teachers feel supported.

If we expect instruction to be responsive and culturally sustaining, we must ask:

Do our systems truly prioritize safety or just the appearance of performance?

The Leadership Mirror

As school leaders, we are the tone-setters. How we lead becomes the emotional rhythm others move to.

When we model calm in the face of pressure, we permit teachers to do the same with their students. That starts with pausing instead of panicking...naming the tension but not feeding it.

When we lead with transparency, we build trust not through perfection, but through clarity. That might sound like:

"Here's what we know, here's what we're still figuring out, and here's how we'll decide."

When we are decisive in defending student wellness, equity, and staff sustainability, we empower teachers to trust their voice in the classroom. When they know we'll back them, they can lead with courage—not caution.

Trust is not a side effect of leadership; it's a prerequisite. And **permission** is its first fruit.

Permission, Presence, and Psychological Safety

Neither students nor adults will fully engage in community, creativity, or challenge until they know they have that permission. They won't contribute meaningfully until they know they're not just being managed; they're being led with integrity.

That permission is felt in the smallest of moments:

When a teacher takes a creative risk and isn't penalized if it flops.

When a student discloses something hard, they are met with belief instead of judgment.

When a staff member brings forward a concern and sees it turned into action.

As leaders, we must constantly ask:

Are the people I lead holding their breath? Or have I created the conditions for a collective exhale?

Beneath every lesson plan and staff agenda is an unwritten curriculum, one that teaches people whether they are safe to show up fully.

This legacy seed reminds us that trust is not just something we talk about; it's something we feel. When students are in survival mode and can't leave their invisible knapsack at the door, learning and collaboration take a backseat to self-protection.

As school leaders, our responsibility is to build the psychological safety that allows authenticity, belonging, and growth to take root...for everyone.

Reflection Journal Starter:

Trust doesn't begin with a mission statement or a strategic plan; it begins with the feeling that it's safe to exhale. In schools, that kind of psychological safety is cultivated long before a lesson is taught. It's built through daily signals:

The tone a leader sets in meetings.

The consistency of a leader's actions.

The systems they shape to support, not control

The people they lead.

Reflection Prompt:

Are the people you lead holding their breath, or have you created the conditions for a collective exhale?

Legacy Seed in Action:

Create regular opportunities for students to provide anonymous feedback to you regarding whether they feel physically and psychologically safe in school. Share back with them what you've learned and take visible steps to respond to their concerns. When students see that their voices don't just enter a box, their trust will deepen.

Legacy Checkpoint:

Leadership shapes the hidden curriculum: the unspoken lessons about trust, safety, and belonging. When you lead with presence, clarity, and care, you do more than support instruction—you help others breathe more freely. And that breath? That's where growth begins.

Chapter Two Closing Reflection: Trust Is the Thread That Holds It All Together

"Once trust is built, the most powerful thing a leader can do is show up; fully, consistently, and humanely."

– Legacy-Driven Leadership.

Leadership begins with vision, but it only moves forward through trust.

This chapter explored how trust takes shape in schools. Not just as an abstract value, but as an everyday practice.

We began with the **foundation** that communication is only as strong as the trust that carries it. Without trust, even the clearest message will fail to land. Words lose weight. Vision stays stuck on paper.

We then faced a harder truth that **no strategy, no matter how thoughtful, can outrun a deficit of trust.** Change only moves at the speed people feel safe enough to follow.

From there, we turned inward. We examined the **role of mutual trust**, not just from team to leader, but from leader to team. We emphasized that leaders can't ask others to trust them if they aren't willing to extend it first. Leadership modeling matters.

Finally, we returned to the classroom to understand that **the trust you build with your staff becomes the soil where student safety grows.** When educators feel seen, supported, and anchored in a culture of sincerity and decisive care, that trust ripples. It reaches students. It transforms learning spaces.

Before moving on, pause to reflect:

Are you building bridges or unintentionally burning them?

Are your actions reinforcing safety or creating silent distance?

Does your leadership invite permission or merely compliance?

Trust isn't a leadership technique. It's the hidden curriculum your school absorbs every day.

It's the legacy you shape in moments seen and unseen. And once trust is built, the most powerful thing a leader can do is show up fully, consistently, and humanely.

Trust is the legacy you leave long after the strategies fade.

Chapter Three - The Presence Principle: Leading with Humanity at the Center

Once trust is built, the most powerful thing a leader can do is show up; fully, consistently, and humanely.

Leadership isn't about titles. It's about presence. In the rhythm of a school day, it's easy to get swept away by paperwork, pressure, or politics. But the heartbeat of leadership doesn't live in the office. It lives in the hallways, the classrooms, and the conversations in between.

This chapter explores the power of authentic presence; how being physically and emotionally available builds trust, strengthens relationships, and centers the people who make schools thrive.

It's about showing up not just to observe, but to connect. To cultivate the hum of a school aligned in purpose. To ask how staff are *really* doing. To greet students by name and build a community where authenticity lives.

Presence isn't just a leadership habit; it's a leadership stance.

These pages reflect a core belief: that people come before paperwork. That vision only takes root through relational trust. And that leadership, at its core, is human work—grounded in dignity, connection, and care. When leaders are visible, intentional, and people-centered, they don't just lead a school.

They lead a culture.

Legacy Seeds in This Chapter:

- **Cultivate the Hum** – *Find the rhythm of a connected, aligned culture.*

- **Community Begins Where Authenticity Lives** – *Trust grows in realness, not performance.*

- **The Importance of Building Relational Trust** –*Presence gives vision meaning.*

- **Make Yourself Visible** – *Leadership is felt, not just seen.*

Legacy Seed: Cultivate the Hum

"Not the noise. Not the chaos. Not the scattered applause from a few high-performing classrooms. The hum."

– Legacy-Driven Leadership.

There's a low, steady rhythm that tells you your school is aligned, even in the quiet.

As school leaders, we often feel pressure to amplify the bright spots or rush to extinguish fires. But true leadership lives in the *spaces between*. It lives in the *rhythm* you help to sustain; the quiet, consistent signals that trust is high, systems are clear, and people are rowing in the same direction.

The hum is what happens when culture becomes the air your team breathes. You don't have to announce it. You can feel it.

You hear it when a teacher walks into their classroom with a calm confidence, trusting that they're supported. You hear it when staff across grade levels begin to use a shared language around academics and belonging. You hear it when hallway check-ins, morning meetings, and moments with paraprofessionals carry presence, not just procedure. It's subtle, but unmistakable.

What If You're Not Hearing the Hum Yet?

What if you're only catching faint echoes in isolated corners of your building?

This is where leadership becomes transformative. When

excellence shows up in pockets, your job isn't just to celebrate it, it's to study it.

Ask yourself:

Why is this working here?

What conditions (structures, relationships, mindsets) are allowing it to flourish?

Your task is to observe with curiosity, not control. After observing, begin to translate those insights gained. This is not to duplicate every move; it's to honor the essence of what's working and adapt to fit new contexts.

The goal isn't uniformity. It's resonance. Every classroom and space should sound different, but each should feel part of the same pulse. And the pulse...that hum...is a sign that your culture isn't scattered. It's synced.

Leaning Toward the Hum

This kind of alignment doesn't happen by accident. It requires intentional and consistent leadership; leaders who know that consistency is not the enemy of creativity, it's the soil that it grows from. Leaders who understand that sustainability is quieter than a highlight reel.

When you find yourself hearing those faint notes of promise, don't stop at appreciation. Lean in. Lift it. Build structures around it. Cultivate it. Share the learning. Protect the time. And keep going until the applause becomes a hum of shared excellence. Strong leadership isn't always loud; it's felt. And it echoes long after the spotlight fades.

Reflection Journal Starter

Every school has moments of brilliance; those quiet, steady pulses of excellence that hum beneath the surface but signal deep alignment. But the hum doesn't emerge by accident. It's cultivated through intentional leadership, thoughtful observation, and commitment to shared learning. When leaders go beyond celebrating isolated success and begin identifying the deeper conditions that made it possible, they help turn bright spots into a *shared rhythm*. The goal isn't to replicate; it's to resonate. Legacy-driven leadership is built not through control, but through coherence.

Reflection Question:

What would it look like to shift from celebrating isolated success to building shared momentum, where the hum of excellence becomes the heartbeat of your entire school?

Legacy Seed in Action:

Highlight one classroom this week as a "bright spot" and arrange for teachers to conduct a learning walk to that classroom to visit and observe. Ask those visiting teachers to identify what created the "hum" of learning and to share one insight that they can bring back to their own practice. When bright spots are amplified, the hum spreads.

Legacy Checkpoint:

Legacy-driven leadership turns sparks into systems.
It doesn't just celebrate bright spots:

It studies them.

It scales them.

It sustains them.

Your legacy lives not in the loudest moments,
but in the quiet, consistent hum of a school moving with shared purpose.

(We will revisit this concept in Chapter 6.)

Legacy Seed: Community Begins Where Authenticity Lives

"A strong school isn't built on slogans—it's built on truth. And truth requires space for people to show up fully."

– Legacy-Driven Leadership.

Strong school communities don't happen by accident. They are built one honest, intentional relationship at a time.

It's easy to name culture as a strategic priority. It's harder still to live it as a daily practice. The truth is this:

Without authentic relationships, there is no real community. And without community, there is no sustainable change.

The Tone Starts with You

As a school leader, you set the tone. Your words matter - but your presence matters more.

Every interaction, every decision, every hallway conversation sends a message about what you value. The same can be true of the people you pass by; the staff member you haven't checked in on, the parent you overlook at dismissal, the custodian whose work you never publicly acknowledge.

If you want students to show up fully, you must model that courage. If you want families to trust your leadership, that trust must be earned through presence, consistency, and follow-through.

If you want your staff to commit to shared work, they first have to believe that they matter, not just as professionals, but as people.

Authenticity vs. Performance

Authenticity and performance can look the same on the surface, but they *feel* quite different to the people experiencing them.

Performative Leadership	Authentic Leadership
Checks boxes.	**Builds bridges.**
Shows up at events because they "should".	**Stays present because they care.**
Talks about inclusion.	**Lives it by listening, adjusting, and centering those most often unheard.**
Compliance-based initiatives without follow-up.	**Efforts rooted in relationships, trust-building, and sustainability.**

When leadership is performative, people may comply, but they won't connect. They might smile, but they won't speak up. They might attend meetings, but they won't bring their whole selves to the work. The focus is on compliance over connection.

What Authentic Leadership Creates

Authentic leadership creates psychological safety. It sends a message that:

Students are more than test scores.

Families are more than data points.

Teachers are more than their job titles.

This kind of leadership isn't about charisma; it's about consistency. It asks you to show up even when the work is hard. To admit when you don't know. To learn out loud.

Authenticity doesn't mean perfection. It means alignment. It indicates who you are when no one's watching, matches who you are when everyone is. That alignment is what turns a leader into a **trusted presence**, not just a visible one.

So don't confuse proximity with presence. Don't mistake announcements for connection. Don't let performance substitute for purpose.

If your goal is to build a school community that lasts, start by asking:

Where am I being real?

Where am I just playing the part?

The most enduring cultures aren't built on showmanship or slogans. They're built on trust, truth, and the quiet power of showing up human.

Start with presence. Lead with purpose. Build with authenticity.

Authenticity sets the foundation, but presence is what gives your vision life. A vision, no matter how compelling, won't move your school unless it's grounded in trust and lived through relationships.

Reflection Journal Starter

A strong school community is more than a value statement; it's a daily commitment. And the work of building it starts with you.

Not with a strategy. Not with a survey. With your presence, consistency, and authenticity.

When people know you're showing up for them and not just the role, you shift the culture from guarded compliance to genuine connection. That's how transformation begins. Through honest relationships that honor people as they are, not just as we need them to be.

Reflection Prompt:

How can your leadership create a culture where authenticity is not just allowed, but expected, affirmed, and sustained for every member of your school community?

What impact might your authenticity (or lack of it) be having on the trust within your school community?

Legacy Seed in Action:

Share a personal leadership challenge with your team at your next meeting and explain to them what you learned from it. Keep it honest and specific; being vulnerable opens the door for others to do the same.

Legacy Checkpoint:

Legacy-driven leadership begins where perfection ends. When you shed the need to appear perfect and choose to lead with presence, people respond with trust. That trust becomes the foundation of community. *Authenticity doesn't just make you visible; it makes you believable.*

That belief is what makes transformation possible.

Legacy Seed: The Importance of Building Relational Trust

"A bold vision statement won't change your school; your presence that drives the credibility of your vision will."

– *Legacy-Driven Leadership.*

You can craft the most inspiring mission statement, the most beautifully worded set of school core values, and print your goals across every hallway bulletin board, but if the people in your building don't feel those values lived out through your presence as a school leader, it's just a poster.

The Difference Between Words and Weight

Vision alone doesn't build momentum. It doesn't establish culture. It doesn't inspire lasting change or impact. The real work only starts when the people in your care trust that your messaging is more than words; that it's something that they can see, feel, and believe *through their daily interactions with you.* You cannot move a school forward from behind closed doors. You can't lead a culture of connection without first being connected yourself.

Students don't follow posters. They follow people they trust, people they see, people who see them.

That's the part that we sometimes miss as school leaders. We're charged with implementing the school vision. We revisit it during meetings and highlight it during our walkthroughs. A well-crafted message, however, doesn't create the intended movement if relationships beneath the messaging aren't strong enough to carry it forward.

Presence is the great translator of a school vision. It's what makes values visible. It's what turns theory into culture.

What Presence Really Means

Let's be clear...presence is not about proximity. It's not about being seen walking the hallways or checking boxes on your mental "visibility log". It's not enough to just be in the building; it's about *how* you show up. It's about the quality of your interactions, not just the quantity.

Are you accessible? Are you grounded in listening? Are you available when it matters the most? Do your actions align with the values that you push?

Every moment you're authentically present, you are reinforcing that your leadership is rooted in something deeper than your title and position. It's rooted in purpose, not performance.

Presence is what gives your vision legs. It's one of the most underutilized leadership tools. It costs nothing but means everything. Without presence, there can be no trust. Without trust, the words won't stick. Without relationships, the work won't scale.

Before you roll out your next initiative, ask:

Have I earned the kind of trust that makes the vision believable?

Have I invested in the relationships that will give our message meaning?

The real test of your vision isn't whether a fancy quote is printed in every classroom. It's whether it's *felt* in those classrooms, in the hallways, and through every decision that you make as a school leader. When your **presence** reflects your **purpose**, and your being is grounded in **trust**, your **leadership** becomes **more than a slogan**. It becomes a promise, one that is carried forward by the people you serve.

Once that trust is built, the most powerful thing a leader can do is show up; fully, authentically, consistently, and humanely. That's how a poster becomes a culture, and vision becomes legacy.

Reflection Journal Starter

"Vision-casting", the art of articulating a strong and compelling picture of the future, is often treated as a leader's first and boldest move. Truth is, it doesn't become real until it's rooted in trust. A powerful message won't matter if your presence doesn't reflect it, and people won't follow a purpose they haven't seen you live.

Relationships are what give vision weight. They're what transform written words into shared belief. And it's not the mission on the wall that shapes culture. It's how leadership shows up in the day-to-day.

Reflection Question:

How are your daily leadership actions reinforcing or contradicting the vision you've set? Are your relationships strong enough to carry your message forward? How do you know?

Legacy Seed in Action:

Use the last few minutes of your next meeting for one-on-one check-ins with individual staff members. Focus not just on what they are doing, but also on how they're doing. Continue this practice regularly so that staff see that trust is being built through consistent, relational moments, not in grand gestures.

Legacy Checkpoint:

Legacy-driven leadership is lived, not laminated. Legacy-driven leaders don't just launch vision statements; they live them.

Your presence is what brings your vision to life. When

your presence reflects your purpose, your vision becomes more than words; it becomes a promise.

Let your presence be the loudest part of your vision.

Legacy Seed: Make Yourself Visible

"Leadership is presence. Not just in meetings, but in hallways, classrooms, and moments that matter. Build credibility through visibility."

– Legacy-Driven Leadership.

After vision is grounded in trust, what comes next is how you live it out. That begins with being seen not just by title, but through action, empathy, and presence.

Visibility is more than just showing up. It's about how you show up and who you're showing up for.

Leadership is never defined by a title or how someone is positioned to be in front of a room. True leadership – the kind that shapes a culture and earns credibility - is defined by what people feel when you enter a space, and what lingers when you leave. This type of leadership requires more than positional authority. It demands **relational credibility**. It calls for presence that connects, not presence that performs.

You can't shortcut your way to trust. You can't micromanage your way into belonging. Leadership centered on people demands more than visibility as a routine. It demands visibility as a relationship. Being seen isn't enough. You must be felt. You must be known—not for your position and title, but for your presence.

From Presence to Practice

People-centered practice starts with presence. It means leading from the hallways, not just the office. It means pausing to check in, not just walking by. It means honoring humanity before hierarchy...**every single day**. True visibility shows up when it's the least convenient:

When a teacher is on the verge of burnout and needs more than a strategy, they need a leader who listens without rushing.

When a classroom is in chaos, you choose not to avoid it but enter it without blame.

When a teacher provides hard feedback, and instead of becoming defensive, you respond with reflection.

These moments are the heartbeat of visibility. Not just the morning greeting, the everyday choices to stay present, especially when the work gets hard.

Visibility also calls for *equity*. It's not enough to show up where you're comfortable. Your leadership must reach those who are traditionally ignored:

The students who don't speak your language.

The staff who often go unacknowledged—paraprofessionals, night custodians, bus drivers.

The families who don't know all the protocols but are trusting you with what matters most.

This is what it means to shift from positional presence to relational visibility and from transactional leadership to transformational presence. Positional presence often stops at being seen. It's transactional and impermanent; a checkmark that says, "the leader showed up."

Relational visibility goes further; it's transformational because the people in your charge don't just see you, they feel you. They experience your presence as trust, consistency, and care.

Positional Presence	Relational Visibility
Leading from your office.	Leading from hallways, the cafeteria, the carline, and the tough conversations.
Leading inconsistently.	Leading with consistency, empathy, and intention.
Leadership that is merely visible.	Leadership that is felt.

You lead not just from the office but from the hallways,

the cafeteria, the carline, the tough conversations, the shared celebrations. You lead with consistency, with empathy, and with intention. Jack (2023) found that consistent, high-quality principal visibility directly boosted teacher trust and morale. That kind of presence can't be reduced to a performance; it's leadership that is felt.

Some days, it might look like a rolling desk so you can complete your tasks while staying connected to the rhythm of the building. Other days, it looks like a strategic no to reclaim time with people over paperwork. Every system you design and every decision you make touches *real people*. Every moment you lead, you're either building a connection or distancing from it. Leadership that is merely visible gets noticed.

Leadership that is felt gets followed.

So don't just be seen. Be available. Be consistent. Be human.

That's what makes your leadership real.

That's what makes your presence matter.

Reflection Journal Starter

Leadership isn't just about being seen; it's about being felt. Visibility without connection quickly becomes performance. When you move through your building with purpose and people in mind, your presence becomes a form of care.

Being visible means stepping into the spaces where others live their day-to-day: hallways, classrooms, lunchrooms…and showing up not just as a supervisor, but as a partner. Presence that is personal, inclusive, and consistent tells your team:

"I see you. I value you. I'm in this with you."

Reflection Prompt:

Where does your leadership show up consistently? Where might your presence still be missing?

How can a school leader shift from being seen to being felt across the entire school community?

Legacy Seed in Action:

Choose a daily transition (e.g., arrival, lunch, dismissal) to be fully present this week. Engage with students and staff in that moment without your phone in your hand. Over time, rotate which transition you choose so that your presence is felt throughout the building during the different rhythms of the school day.

Legacy Checkpoint:

Impermanence is a reminder that everything we build has an expiration date. Titles shift, programs change, and even the strongest initiatives eventually evolve. Transactional leadership leans into that impermanence. It manages tasks for the moment but *leaves no roots*. When the leader moves on, so does the progress.

Transformational leadership, however, embraces impermanence by planting what will outlast us: trust, culture, and capacity. These are the seeds that remain when the job title is gone.

Legacy-driven leaders don't just walk the halls; they shape the culture by *how* they walk through them. Your presence becomes your promise when it is consistent, human, and rooted in care. Remain visible, stay connected, and you will be the transformative leader your people need.

Visibility without connection is just a show.

Chapter Three Closing Reflection: The Presence Principle

"Once trust is built, the most powerful thing a leader can do is show up— fully, consistently, and humanely. But showing up is only the beginning. Growth comes next...and growth doesn't happen by chance; it happens by choice."

– Legacy-Driven Leadership.

Presence is more than proximity. It's the daily choice to show up with purpose and authenticity, not just in position and authority.

When leaders prioritize people over process, relationships over routines, and visibility over performance, they create the conditions where trust grows, and culture takes root. Centering your leadership on relationships doesn't mean lowering expectations. It means anchoring those expectations with care. With clarity. And with a commitment to seeing the humanity in every member of your school community.

Sustainable change doesn't begin with mandates; it begins with presence.

Every hallway conversation, classroom visit, or family meeting leaves more than a message. It leaves a mark. Like a leaf pressed gently into wet cement, your presence leaves impressions that, over time, shape the story of your school.

Those impressions become culture.

They become your legacy.

Leadership that honors presence is the kind of leadership that lasts.

Chapter Four: Growth and Accountability

Growth doesn't happen by accident; it's cultivated through awareness, courage, and consistency.

This chapter explores what it means to move a school forward without losing sight of the people within it. It invites leaders to reflect honestly, act with integrity, and stretch beyond what's comfortable. True growth isn't about doing more; it's about doing what matters, with clarity.

Clarity begins when you pause to observe, zooming out from the urgency to see the patterns that shape your culture.
Whether you're guiding from the front, walking alongside your team, or stepping onto the balcony for a clearer view, each leadership posture carries power. Each moment of reflection becomes a mirror. And each act of courage becomes a message to your school community:

We're just not here to improve. We're here to transform.

In this chapter, we focus on leadership that:

Seeks perspective before action,

Practices reflection before reaction, and

Grounds itself in purpose before goals.

In legacy-driven leadership, progress isn't just measured by outcomes; it's revealed in how intentionally we grow.

Legacy Seeds in This Chapter:

- **Views from the Balcony** – *Finding clarity through intentional perspective.*

- **Students Rise When Adults Reflect** – *Honoring growth that begins with us.*

- **Leaders Shape What They Allow** – *Confronting what persists in our silence.*

- **Changing the World Starts with How We Lead** – *Choosing conviction over comfort.*

- **Before Goals, Feed Your Spirit** – *Grounding yourself before guiding others.*

- **All Good Work Is Worthy of Dedication** – *Staying rooted when resistance shows up.*

Legacy Seed: Views From the Balcony

"You can't lead if you never pause to see the full picture. Step back. Reflect. Then act."

– Legacy-Driven Leadership.

Leadership isn't about staying in the mix. It's about knowing when to engage, when to observe, and when to rise above the moment to see the whole picture.

In the rhythm of school life, it's easy to confuse movement with meaning. The pace is relentless. You move from crisis to crisis, from meeting to meeting, email to email; always reacting and always responding. The motion never stops. The constant motion doesn't equal clarity and quickly becomes exhaustion.

That's why I often return to the metaphor from Ronald Heifetz's leadership work: *The Dance Floor and the Balcony.*

On the dance floor, you're immersed in the action; you're close to the pulse but clouded by the noise. You respond to what's loudest but not always the necessary. You lead from the middle of the room, but you can't always see what's happening in the corners. You remain reactive, hoping clarity will catch up to your pace.

Sometimes, to lead clearly, you need a new vantage point.

When you step onto the balcony, your perspective shifts. The blur becomes a pattern.

You begin to see who's dancing and who's left standing alone. You notice where energy decreases and where it's leaking. You see which systems are aligned with your vision and which ones are quietly undermining it. From this higher vantage point, the dynamics of your school come into sharper focus:

Which grade level teams are thriving, and which are quietly unraveling?

Who is heard and who is constantly overlooked?

Where are your most vulnerable students falling through the cracks, and why?

The balcony isn't a retreat from your responsibilities of leadership. It's a return to it – with greater clarity. It equips you to reenter it with intention, strategy, and clarity. You begin to lead with an alignment between your values, your systems, your people, and your mission. You stop spinning in response to noise and start moving in rhythm with what matters most.

It doesn't mean stepping away from people. It means honoring the work enough to lead it wisely.

Many leaders feel guilty creating space to reflect. They worry they'll appear disengaged or out of touch. But the most trusted leaders know when to pause. They know that clarity requires distance. They understand that leadership isn't just about being in the room; it's about knowing what's happening *because* you took time to see the full picture.

Equity lives in these moments of perspective.

From the balcony, you can notice the subtle, but powerful patterns of inclusion and exclusion:

Who's always invited to the table?

Whose silence goes unchecked?

Where do certain students feel invisible, while others always receive the benefit of the doubt?

You cannot shift what you cannot see. And you cannot see what you're unwilling to step back and examine. Once you examine these patterns of inequity, you can begin to ask why these patterns exist, who is responsible for these patterns existing, and what can be done about them.

Make balcony time part of your weekly rhythm. Schedule it. Honor it. Guard it. Even just 20 minutes of structured reflection each week can change how you lead on the floor. When you come down from the balcony, come back with a deeper question than, "What's next?"

Ask:

What's needed now, based on what I've seen, heard, and felt?

Legacy-driven leaders don't just stay in motion. They rise above it, learn from it, and return with clarity, courage, and care. The balcony isn't where you escape the work. It's where you learn to lead it better. Balcony time isn't a luxury. It's a leadership discipline.

Reflection Journal Starter

Leadership requires both motion and **intentional pause**. The balcony offers a vital vantage point:

A place to step back, notice the rhythm, and make sense of what's unfolding.

Without that perspective, leaders risk becoming reactive rather than reflective; caught in the noise of daily demands and missing the deeper patterns underneath. But when you build balcony time into your leadership rhythm, you create space for clarity, not just about your team, but about yourself.

From that higher view, you notice what is usually missed: the subtle gaps, unspoken tensions, implicit bias, and unseen possibilities that can only be observed from above. You see the dance and the disconnect. The energy and the exclusion.

It's not about pulling away from the work. It's about returning to it with deeper wisdom and renewed intention.

Reflection Prompt:

What perspectives, patterns, or possibilities are waiting for you at the balcony? How will you use them to reenter the work with clarity, courage, and care?

Legacy Seed in Action:

Intentionally step out of day-to-day tasks for one hour to review your school's culture from a strategic perspective. Look for patterns in how students and staff interact with each other, how decisions are communicated, and how values show up in practice. Afterwards, identify one insight that you will take back to the "dance floor" to help guide your daily leadership decisions.

Legacy Checkpoint:

Legacy-driven leadership requires both **proximity and perspective.**

From the floor, you build trust through connection.

From the balcony, you build insight through reflection.

When you return to the floor, you don't just react, you realign.

The most impactful leaders know when to engage and when to rise. They don't just lead with motion; they lead with meaning.

Legacy Seed: Students Rise When Adults Reflect

"The best school leaders don't just look out of the window; they look in the mirror."

– Legacy-Driven Leadership.

Before the data dives, performance metrics, professional development plans, and school improvement goals, lasting transformation begins somewhere quieter. It begins with reflection. That reflection starts with the courage to ask the hard questions...not about students, faculty, or other stakeholders, but about ourselves:

What's my role in the patterns that I keep noticing?

What behaviors or dynamics have I unintentionally allowed to take root?

Am I contributing to the very problems that I've been trying to solve?

This mindset shift, from blame to ownership, from reaction to reflection, is where true leadership begins. When something isn't working in a school, the most powerful question a school leader can ask isn't, *"What's wrong with them?"* It's *"What might my leadership be allowing, avoiding, or reinforcing?"*

School leadership is a mirror, not a megaphone.

Your words matter, but your reflection shapes school culture more than the amplification of your voice ever could.

You can talk about equity. You can promote expectations. But if your daily choices don't align with what you claim that you stand for, your leadership loses traction. Staff may comply, but they won't trust. Students may behave, but they won't grow.

When we step back as leaders, we gain perspective. But when we look inward, we gain integrity. Integrity is what builds trust that lasts.

Self-aware leadership sounds like this:

What signals did I miss this week?

What assumptions am I carrying?

How does my bias show up in my decisions?

How might my leadership be experienced in ways that I don't expect or intend?

This kind of self-inquiry doesn't just foster insight; it models accountability.

When adults reflect openly and honestly, something shifts across the culture. Staff begin to speak with more candor. Students notice that listening, not lecturing, is part of the leadership practice. Families start to see a school that grows with them, not despite them.

Reflection isn't just a mindset; it's a skill. A skill that requires:

Intention - *carving out protected time to step back and examine your leadership practices regularly.*

Humility – *a willingness to sit with discomfort and use it as data; and*

Accountability – *systems that invite feedback, document learning, and connect reflection to action.*

This isn't something that school leaders should have to do alone. District offices and leadership teams should build structures that normalize school leader reflection; planning protocols that ask reflective questions, evaluation cycles that invite perspective, and coaching that reinforces the power of pause.

When adults take the time to reflect, they don't just improve, they transform.

And that transformation radiates.

Students rise because we've shown them how. We've done the work on ourselves. We've changed the temperature. We've made the mirror part of the mission.

School culture doesn't shift at the surface; it shifts at the root. And the root is always leadership.

Reflection Journal Starter

Leadership invites action, but it also requires introspection.
In the fast pace of school life, it's easy to focus outward: on staff performance, student behavior, or parent concerns. But real change begins inward, with the courage to pause, reflect, and ask the harder questions of ourselves.

When leaders treat reflection as a leadership discipline, it creates a ripple effect, opening space for honesty, clarity, and growth. From that inward lens, your leadership shifts from reactive to responsive, from performative to principled.

When adults reflect with integrity, school culture doesn't just shift, it deepens. When school leaders model reflection, they create the conditions needed for collective teacher efficacy, the belief that together, staff can directly influence outcomes (Lisi and Frieson, 2025). Growth rises when reflection takes root.

Reflection Prompt:

What might your leadership be allowing, avoiding, or reinforcing? How will honest reflection guide your next step forward?

Legacy Seed in Action:

Schedule a debrief with one teacher about how recent instructional changes have impacted their students. Focus the conversation on what the students are experiencing, where student growth is evident, and where adjustments might help. End the debrief by reflecting together on one insight to carry forward.

Legacy Checkpoint:

Legacy-driven leadership is rooted in self-awareness. It grows not from the spotlight, but from the mirror. Every outward transformation begins with inward truth.

When adults reflect, students rise by example.

That's how school culture changes from the root, not just the surface.

Legacy Seed: Leaders Shape What They Allow

"If you let it happen, you're leading it—whether you meant to or not."

– Legacy-Driven Leadership.

In school leadership, silence is never neutral. It might feel like you're stepping back to promote autonomy, allowing teachers to lead their classrooms, giving grade-level teams or departments the space to operate independently. It might even feel like respect. But over time, **patterns can emerge**. And when those patterns go unacknowledged, your silence begins to carry a different weight. It becomes something else entirely: *permission*.

A teacher yells at a student, and no one steps in. A biased remark slides by in the faculty room. An unfair grading policy or exclusionary practice gets implemented quietly. And no one says a word. These aren't isolated moments. They become the undercurrent of school culture, defining what is tolerated, what is normalized, and what ultimately shapes the student experience.

In truth, the school culture you're trying to build and cultivate is being shaped in real time by what you choose to address.

I remember a summer leadership professional development session on embedding restorative practices into our school's discipline model. During a debrief, a colleague, who didn't agree with restorative practices, turned to me and stated, "Why don't you just send those kids home?" She followed that rhetorical question with,

"Now I have to be a social worker? What are you allowing to continue through your inaction?" She was referring to using restorative practices instead of immediately sending a student home. She equated restorative practices with inaction.

At first, I was taken aback. I knew that restorative practices weren't about removing accountability. I knew the impact of balancing grace with consequence, support with structure.

Her question, although asked out of frustration and was inappropriate, still gave me pause.

Regardless of how I felt in the moment, I knew that I had to sit with that question and think about the best way to respond. Transformational leadership doesn't begin with blame. It begins with honesty. It begins with owning your role in what's allowed to persist. We don't just lead with what we say. We lead with what we endorse through silence. I chose not to be silent in that moment with my colleague and responded accordingly.

It's important to remember that when you speak up with clarity, you model courage. When you act with alignment, you reinforce trust. When you lead with integrity, people follow—not out of fear, but out of belief.

Take a moment. Write down a practice or pattern you're currently tolerating; something that contradicts the culture you're trying to build. Fold the note. Keep it visible. And commit to addressing it within 30 days. Revisit the note, and ask:

What changed because I chose to lead differently?

Leadership isn't just about crafting a vision. It's about holding space for vision accountability.

That's how legacy is built, not only by what you inspire, but by what you're willing to interrupt.

Reflection Journal Starter

Sometimes leadership means holding up the mirror, especially when the reflection is uncomfortable. This seed challenges you to look beyond what's said in your school and focus on what you're silently permitting.

Culture isn't just built by your vision statements or expectations. It's shaped by what goes unchecked, unstated, and unresolved.

When we avoid confrontation, delay hard conversations, or let misalignment linger, we may feel we're keeping the peace, but in reality, we may be disrupting progress.

Legacy-driven leadership requires the courage to act in alignment with your values, even when it's inconvenient, unpopular, or emotionally taxing.

Reflect on how your inaction may be unintentionally shaping the culture you've committed to change and how a single moment of clarity can become a turning point for trust, equity, and transformation.

Reflection Prompt:

What are you currently tolerating that contradicts the culture you say that you value? What intentional step can you take to address it?

Legacy Seed in Action:

Identify one tolerated behavior that undermines your vision. This week, address it directly, whether through a candid conversation, a reset of expectations, or a change in systems. Leadership is revealed in what we refuse to allow, not just in what we encourage.

Legacy Checkpoint:

Every inaction is a decision. The culture you're building is shaped not just by what you lead, but *by what you let linger*. School culture is shaped in the quiet moments, when no one is watching, and in the moments of decision when silence would be easier than action. Your legacy will be defined not only by what you built, but also by what you were brave enough to challenge.

Legacy-driven leadership doesn't just speak truth. It confronts the quiet.

Legacy Seed: Changing the World Starts with How We Lead

"Leadership is a daily act of courage. Change begins in the mirror."

– Legacy-Driven Leadership.

We don't just shape school culture through what we say; we shape it through what we allow.

That was the hard truth of the last legacy seed. But once we face what we've permitted, there comes a new challenge:

Will we lead differently?

Changing the culture of a school is about more than stopping harmful patterns. It's about modeling a better path.

That begins with how we lead.

Leadership isn't proven when things are easy; it's tested in the moments that stretch our patience and demand our convictions. And for today's school leaders, those moments are constant.

You're implementing change while absorbing community fears. You're defending inclusion while balancing strained budgets. You're trying to protect every child's dignity while navigating deeply political terrain.

These are more than logistical challenges. They're moral ones. They demand more than technical expertise. They require clarity, courage, and conscience.

Leadership that changes the world doesn't begin with a program or policy; it begins with a decision. It's the decision to lead with integrity, even when it's inconvenient. To align your actions with your values, even when it costs you something. To stay rooted in your "why," especially when it would be easier to retreat.

You can't advocate for equity while ignoring bias in your own building. You can't champion inclusion while staying silent when students are harmed. You can't lead others through a crisis when you're not grounded in purpose yourself.

Reflection in Action

Legacy-driven leadership is a reflection in action. It's the daily discipline of asking hard questions:

What hard truth am I avoiding?

Whose voices are missing from this decision?

Where am I compromising values over approval or ease?

Leadership isn't about perfection. It's about persistence

to stay aligned with your purpose, especially when it's inconvenient.

Leading through a crisis demands emotional endurance. Advocating for equity demands intellectual humility. And leading with moral courage asks you to move, even when the crowd hesitates.

It won't always be easy. It won't always be safe. It certainly won't always be popular.

The work of transformation was never about popularity. It's about people. It's about justice, It's about legacy. And when you consistently choose courage over comfort, you send a message that ripples far beyond your school walls:

That change is possible.

That leadership matters.

That you are leading in a way that will outlast you.

The culture your school lives by tomorrow is being written by how you choose to lead it today.

Reflection Journal Starter

The work of school leadership is no longer just

operational. It's deeply personal, deeply political, and deeply moral.

Each day, you face decisions that go far beyond schedules and policies. You're navigating tensions around identity, justice, and equity, often without a road map.

In those moments, you have a choice:

Will you protect comfort or model courage?

Your legacy will not be measured by how well you maintain the status quo. It's measured by your willingness to stretch your values into visible, consistent action, especially when it would be so much easier not to.

Change doesn't begin with a memo. It begins with how you show up when it matters most: grounded in your purpose, steady in your stance, and committed to doing right by the people you serve.

Reflection Prompt:

Where is your leadership being tested right now, and what would it look like to move forward with greater moral courage, not just intention?

<u>Legacy Seed in Action:</u>

Share one example of a leader whose small daily actions inspired large change. Explain why this example resonates with you and connect it to your team's current work. Invite the group to identify a small action that they can take this week to model that same principle.

<u>Legacy Checkpoint:</u>

Changing the world begins with conviction.

For many, **that moment is now**.

Every time you choose to lead with clarity, equity, and courage, especially when it's uncomfortable, you plant the kind of seeds that outlast programs and positions. The world doesn't shift when leaders play it safe. It shifts when they show up fully, boldly, and with purpose.

Legacy Seed: Before Goals, Feed Your Spirit

"Excellence starts on the inside. Take care of your spirit—so you can lead with purpose."

– *Legacy-Driven Leadership.*

Before the spreadsheets. Before the mandates. Before the meetings and measurable outcomes...

Feed your spirit.

Every school leader knows the urgency that comes with a new year. The inbox overflows. The calendar fills. Everyone needs something...immediately. And beneath it all is the relentless push to *produce results*.

But sustainable leadership doesn't begin with goals. It begins with grounding.

If your spirit is depleted, your vision will blur. If your values aren't centered, your leadership will drift. And if you don't protect your inner clarity, you risk becoming a shell of your intended self, with ripple effects that touch not only your professional life but your well-being.

Pause on Purpose

Pause on purpose. Not as a luxury but as a necessity.

Ask yourself:

What will sustain me, not just through the wins, but through the weight of the work?

One of the hardest lessons that I learned in leadership is this:

Balance is not a bonus. It's a responsibility.

What you carry inside inevitably shapes what you cultivate outside.

Leadership grounded in clarity and conviction, rather than pressure and performance, is what transforms school culture. And that transformation starts with how you show up:

In your energy

In your systems

In your trust-building

When your spirit is aligned, your leadership follows.

Five Reflective Anchors to Return To

Here are five reflective anchors to return to, especially when the work gets heavy:

Reconnect with your legacy.

- Why did you step into this work?

- What lineage of leadership are you continuing?

Protect what fuels you.

- What gives you life in your role?

- What reminds you that this work is more than a job?

Align your inner and outer self.

- Are you leading with authenticity or just performing the part?

- Where is your leadership grounded, and where has it drifted?

Notice growth in the quiet.

- Where is progress showing up in small, meaningful ways?

- Are you celebrating the journey, not just the outcome?

Build trust that endures…

- Do students, staff, and families feel safe and seen in your presence?

- What legacy of trust are you cultivating across generations?

These aren't just reflective rituals. They're spiritual anchors; reminders that feeding your spirit is foundational to leading with clarity, care, and conviction.

Let's be honest, school leaders often fail to take the same advice that we give others. But when we skip our grounding, we risk falling into our default mode, making decisions from fear or fatigue, and unintentionally replicating the inequities that we're out to disrupt.

Before the year gets loud, make space for silence. Before the checklists take over, return to what truly matters. The most impactful leadership doesn't rush in. It roots in.

Reflection Journal Prompt

Leadership begins with presence, but it's sustained through nourishment.

It's easy to focus on deadlines, metrics, and mandates... And forget the humanity at the center of it all, including your own.

A depleted leader can't model wholeness.

This legacy seed reminds us that sustainable leadership is rooted in alignment between what you believe, how you show up, and how you care for yourself and others. When your spirit is fed, your leadership deepens. It becomes more authentic, more resilient, and more just.

Reflection Prompt:

What would it look like to lead in a way that nourishes your spirit and honors the humanity of those you serve, not just their outcomes?

Legacy Seed in Action:

Block 20 minutes this week for personal reflection or learning that feeds your leadership spirit. Protect that time and treat it as a non-negotiable. Use it to journal, read something that will stretch your perspective, meditate, or revisit your leadership intentions. The goal isn't productivity, it's renewal. Feeding your spirit strengthens your capacity to show up grounded for others and ensures that your leadership is sustained over time.

Legacy Checkpoint:

Feeding your spirit isn't selfish; it's stewardship. Your legacy doesn't grow from depletion. It grows from grounding. Before you lead others, nurture what leads you.

Legacy Seed: All Good Work Is Worthy of Dedication

"The work is hard. The resistance is real. But your consistency is louder than your critics."

– *Legacy-Driven Leadership.*

When your spirit is rooted, your dedication becomes unstoppable.

Leadership is often measured in outcomes. Data. Deliverables. Deadlines. They dominate the dashboard. But real impact? That's shaped in the dedication you bring to the work, especially when no one's watching.

As a school leader, your presence sets the tone. Your consistency builds trust. Your dedication creates the cultural blueprint for how others show up.

But dedication isn't passive. It's not just sticking with something out of habit. In education, especially when equity is the pursuit, dedication means staying committed to the *discomfort* of truth. It means holding space for resistance without shrinking your mission.

Facing the Data

In my early years as an assistant principal, I confronted my school's disproportionate discipline data. Black male students, particularly those with IEPs, were being removed from class, written up, and excluded from learning spaces at more than double the rate of their white peers for the same behaviors. This data was cited by the state. The patterns were clear.

When I named it, resistance surfaced. Some staff nodded in agreement. Others responded with eye rolls or silence. A few took it as a personal attack. But I stayed in the work. I reminded our team to *"Take this work personal, but not personally."*

In a collaborative effort, we examined every school-level practice and procedure connected to student discipline. We focused on our Tier 1 systems because foundational strategies shape equity.

We developed fidelity checklists. Our school behavioral team conducted walkthroughs and used the data collected from the checklists for structured, building-wide feedback. We asked hard questions about consistency, fairness, and unintended impact.

Slowly, as our practices aligned and discipline data began to shift, even the initial skeptics started to understand that this was never about blame. It was always about ensuring that all students felt a sense of belonging, aligning our practices that connect to student discipline across the building, and identifying areas of growth.

Perfecting our implementation of preventative strategies and restorative practices was never an intended outcome; progress towards implementation was. We focused on the 80% of staff who were open to reflection, trusting that their momentum would influence the rest. Dedication isn't about compliance. It's about a collective commitment to what students truly need.

Dedication as a Strategy

Dedication, in this way, becomes both a stance and a strategy. It tells your team that we are not willing to give up because it's hard; we're staying in it because it's just.

All good work is worthy of dedication. Especially the kind that centers students historically pushed to the margins. When leaders stay grounded in their values, even in the face of pushback, they model what accountability looks like.

Not just to goals, but to people.

The work is sacred. Resistance is real. And your dedication is what carries the legacy forward.

Reflection Journal Starter

Legacy isn't built in a single breakthrough; it's cultivated through daily commitment. Through the quiet moments of showing up when it's hard. Through choosing progress over perfection.

This seed reminds us that what you recommit to, especially when it's uncomfortable, is what shapes the culture around you.

When you push through resistance, advocate for equity, or hold steady belief in work others may not yet understand, your dedication sends a message:

This matters.

In the face of fatigue or indifference, that kind of consistency becomes sacred work.

Reflection Prompt:

What does your dedication, especially in challenging seasons, reveal about what you value, and who you're committed to serving?

Legacy Seed in Action:

Publicly acknowledge a "behind-the-scenes" effort by someone on your admin team this week. Be intentional about going beyond a quick thank you. Name the effort made by the person, highlight the impact, and connect it to the larger mission. Dedication is contagious; when leaders honor the quiet, unseen work, they set a tone that values perseverance and builds a culture where every effort matters.

Legacy Checkpoint:

Dedication isn't just about showing up; it's about staying grounded in your values when the work gets hard. And in education, that kind of commitment doesn't just shift outcomes—it shapes lives, rewrites narratives, and builds cultures where all students can thrive.

Chapter Four Closing Reflection: Growth and Accountability

"*The pursuit of growth means you will eventually meet resistance. The question is—will you be ready to lead anyway?*"

– *Legacy-Driven Leadership.*

Accountability isn't about compliance; it's about commitment. To your values. To your team. To the legacy you're building.

The best leaders know when to lead from the floor and when to rise to the balcony. They understand that presence without perspective leads to reactivity, not reflection. They pause. They zoom out. They seek clarity not just for their schools, but for themselves.

Growth doesn't begin with a checklist; it begins with a mirror.

It's in the quiet courage to ask:

"What am I contributing to the very thing I'm complaining about?"

"Where is my leadership allowing misalignment to persist?"

Transformation doesn't start with blame. It starts with ownership. What you allow shapes the school culture, and silence, especially in the face of inequity, is never neutral. What we ignore becomes permission. What we accept becomes practice.

But reflection alone isn't enough. In moments of crisis or

change, the equity we claim must become the equity we model. And that requires inner clarity.

Before the strategies or spreadsheets, leaders must feed their spirit. What we carry inside shows up in what we build outside. Wholeness isn't optional; it's foundational.

Finally, all good work is worthy of dedication. Especially the kind that reshapes minds, centers students, and challenges systems. Leadership rooted in growth and accountability doesn't happen by accident; it's cultivated with presence, sustained through resistance, and lived out in every quiet choice to return, recommit, and rise again.

Take the balcony view. Feed your spirit. Stay dedicated.

Legacy isn't just a vision; it's a daily decision.

Chapter Five: Courage and Change

Growth determines what's possible; courage tests whether we will act on what we've learned by growing. The next step will be to face the discomfort that comes with true change.

Change is never easy, especially in schools where the familiar often feels safest. But the work of legacy-driven leadership demands more than familiarity. It demands courage.

The courage to name the patterns that no longer serve.

The courage to act when comfort resists disruption.

The courage to believe in change, even when progress is slow or invisible.

In school leadership, courage shows up in quiet moments and in bold decisions. It's found in the uncomfortable conversations, the imperfect first steps, and the long arcs of growth that stretch beyond applause. It's what allows leaders to trade certainty for clarity, perfection for progress, and urgency for sustainability.

Sometimes, in our attempts to change or fix something quickly, we end up uprooting what was already blooming.

As Fred Hammond once sang,

"Thinking my foolishness can meet my needs, pulled up flowers, making room for weeds."

Courageous leadership means slowing down long enough to discern the difference between healing and harming; recognizing when we're tending the garden and when we're unknowingly planting weeds.

Legacy Seeds in This Chapter:

- **The Comfort Zone Is a Beautiful Place** — *where transformation begins by confronting the patterns we protect.*

- **Aim for Success, Not Perfection** — *where we release the myth of flawlessness to lead with humility and presence.*

- **Change Takes Time** — *where we honor process and learn to celebrate the small wins that build momentum.*

- **Strong Schools Aren't Loud, They're Rooted** – *where values guide culture more than volume ever could.*

These legacy seeds call us to reflect on the kind of leadership that doesn't just disrupt but endures. Courageous change doesn't come from force. It comes from alignment, intention, and an unwavering belief that something better is possible and worth fighting for.

Legacy Seed: The Comfort Zone Is a Beautiful Place...

"If you avoid discomfort, you also avoid growth. Legacy lives outside your default setting."

– Legacy-Driven Leadership.

The comfort zone is quiet. Familiar. Predictable.

It's where systems stay unquestioned, routines run on autopilot, and change is postponed in the name of order. It's where the comfort of faculty and staff is often centered over the experiences of students.

But it's also where equity goes to stall.

As school leaders, we often confront resistance not because the work is flawed, but because the work threatens comfort. And when discomfort rises, fear often follows. That fear, left unexamined, pulls educators back into their *default settings*; those ingrained habits and assumptions that feel safe but are often misaligned with the mission of legacy-driven education.

As I shared in the previous chapter, during my early years as a school leader, I challenged the faculty and staff to confront one of our most glaring patterns: the disproportionate discipline data affecting our African American male students. I didn't assign blame to individuals, but I did challenge the collective comfort that allowed those outcomes to persist. The challenge was extended to everyone, from the custodians and paraprofessionals to the school administration, including me.

Examining the policies, practices, and procedures that contributed to the disproportionality was uncomfortable. Questioning when we resorted to our default patterns was uncomfortable. Naming the comforts we clung to – even when they harmed students and families – was uncomfortable.

But we pushed past the silence and asked the hard questions:

What are we allowing?

Who is being harmed?

What are we willing to change?

Naming discomfort isn't enough. Courageous leaders don't just ask tough questions in private; they create conditions for those questions to be asked in the community. They hold space for discomfort without defensiveness and remind the team:

"We're not uncomfortable because we're wrong. We're uncomfortable because we're growing."

To support this, we implemented two key practices:

- **Structured Reflection Protocols**: We built in

regular time for faculty to review patterns in discipline, instruction, and student feedback. But we didn't stop at the data; we asked *what it felt like* to confront it. We named emotions in the room: frustration, guilt, defensiveness, doubt, grief. And we reminded staff that *those feelings were welcome, but not final.*

- **Collective Accountability Circles**: In small cross-functional teams, we examined how our roles contribute to either equity or exclusion. Each conversation ended with the same question:

  - *"What one practice will we shift this week to center the students who've been historically left out?"*

The goal wasn't immediate transformation; it was shared responsibility.

And yes, there was resistance. Growth often sounds like discomfort before it ever sounds like agreement.

Change began when we redefined discomfort not as danger, but as a signpost: *you're on the edge of something important.* When the data began to shift, and more importantly, when student voice and experience improved, that edge became a turning point.

As school leaders, we must recognize when fear is masquerading as routine. We help schools challenge their *default settings*, not for the sake of disruption, but for the sake of growth.

Leadership that remains in the comfort zone cannot transform culture. And culture that doesn't grow stagnates.

Reflection Journal Starter

Every school has a default setting, a way things have always been done. And every leader has a comfort zone. But progress doesn't live there.

This seed reminds us that real change begins when we recognize comfort not just as a personal habit, but as a collective condition that can either protect students or protect the status quo. In equity work, staying comfortable often disguises harm. When school leaders model the courage to step into discomfort, they send a powerful message: growth is not only possible, but also expected.

Discomfort may not feel safe, but it can be sacred. When we choose to disrupt what no longer serves our students, we plant the seeds of transformation.

Reflection Prompt:

Where are you being called to lead your team through discomfort, and what supports will help you stay rooted in that work when resistance rises?

Legacy Seed in Action:

Take one leadership action this week that pushes you into discomfort. This could be a long-avoided conversation, trying a new initiative, or inviting feedback that you may not want to hear. Make note of what you learned. Share one key learning with a colleague or journal your thoughts on this experience and make note of how it might shape your next step.

Legacy Checkpoint:

True leadership is not the avoidance of discomfort; it's guiding your community through it with clarity, care, and courage. Nothing transformative ever came from staying in place. Growth demands discomfort.

Your willingness to lead beyond comfort might be the turning point that rewrites the story for your students, especially those who are historically marginalized.

Legacy Seed: Aim for Success, Not Perfection

"Perfection isn't the goal—progress is. Don't let fear of flaws keep you from leading forward."

– *Legacy-Driven Leadership.*

There is no such thing as a perfect school leader. I know that it may be hard to hear, but it's true. And yet, many of us enter the role tethered to an invisible standard we can never quite reach. It shows up in the quiet pressure we put on ourselves:

To respond to every email with speed and grace

To always find the right words in tense conversations

To make decisions that satisfy everyone

To navigate each moment with polished precision.

Perfectionism doesn't make us better leaders. It keeps us from becoming the kind of leaders our communities truly need. It thrives in environments where image matters more than growth. It silences innovation. It encourages self-censorship. Over time, it creates cultures where mistakes are punished or hidden, where people don't take risks because safety is defined by staying in line.

In a way, perfectionism is just another comfort zone. A polished one. A quiet one. But still a barrier.

In the previous seed, we reflected on how growth often begins with discomfort. This seed continues that challenge. It takes courage to let go of perfection and lead with presence instead. In a field defined by change, human complexity, and urgent needs, perfection simply doesn't fit...

Progress does.

Success in leadership doesn't mean getting everything right the first time. It means moving with intention when things go wrong. It means adjusting with humility, earning publicly, and extending grace to your *team* and *yourself*.

The best leaders don't aim to be flawless. They aim to be grounded. They listen more than they defend. They own their missteps without shame. And they keep going; not because it's easy, but because the work matters.

If we want our schools to be places where students grow through trial, error, reflection, and support, then our leadership must model the same. That starts with releasing the myth of perfection and embracing the deeper work of self-awareness, vulnerability, and steady, values-driven progress.

Your legacy won't be defined by how polished your performance was. Your legacy will be felt in the clarity you brought, the risks you took, and the kind of space you made for others to grow alongside you.

Legacy-driven leadership isn't about being perfect. It's about being present even when it's hard.

Reflection Journal Starter

Perfection may resemble excellence on the surface, but in school leadership, it often hides something deeper: fear. The fear of getting it wrong. The fear of being judged. The fear of being seen as anything less than fully in control.

Leadership isn't a performance. It's a practice. And just like learning, it gets messy.

This seed invites you to release the myth that leadership requires flawlessness. It calls you to reflect not just on how you lead, but *why* you lead and to embrace the imperfections that come with doing the real work of growth, equity, and human connection.

Because when we let go of the need to be perfect, we permit others to grow too.

Reflection Prompt:

Where in your leadership are you holding on too

tightly, striving to control, to polish, to perform, when what's needed is presence, vulnerability, or trust?

Legacy Seed in Action:

Review one current project where you suspect perfectionism is stalling progress. With your team, identify ways in which the focus can shift from flawless execution to meaningful progress that moves the work forward. Then, commit to a concrete next step that reflects this shift from perfection to success.

Legacy Checkpoint:

Perfection seeks control. Legacy seeks connection.

Real leadership means choosing courage over image, reflection over reaction, and growth over ego.

What lasts isn't how perfect you appeared. It's how deeply you showed up and how fully you made space for others to do the same.

Legacy Seed: Change Takes Time

"Change takes time; give yourself permission to celebrate while you wait."

– Legacy-Driven Leadership.

In education, urgency can feel like oxygen; constant, consuming, and non-negotiable. There's always a new initiative to launch, a metric to meet, a crisis to resolve before the next one begins. School leaders are trained to respond quickly, fix immediately, and produce results fast.

In the constant churn of forward motion, school leaders often overlook a quiet truth:

You have to go slow to go fast.

I first heard those words from Jasmine Brown, my supervisor and a mentor during my earliest days as an Assistant Principal. At the time, it felt like a gentle reminder. It wasn't much later that I understood it as a discipline, one rooted in sustainability and the courage to honor process over performance.

This seed is part of a progression:

We named the courage it takes to leave the comfort zone and confront collective defaults.

We dismantled the myth of perfection and reframed success as forward motion, not flawless execution.

Now, we're reminded that change, even when it's

courageous and intentional, takes time.

Deep change, the kind that redefines systems, challenges inequity, and reaches students on the margins, doesn't happen overnight. It unfolds in layers. It requires leaders who are willing to resist the pressure to "prove" and instead stay grounded in building something that lasts.

Maybe you've spent this year facing down challenges that felt immovable:

Opportunity gaps that resisted interventions.

Staff burnout, philosophical divides, or leadership fatigue.

Systemic inequities that either no one else seemed ready to name or completely ignored.

You may have restructured support systems, reimagined discipline practices, or pushed for a more inclusive school culture and still felt like progress was slow or invisible.

But pause. Zoom out. Look again.

That tiered support system that's finally gaining traction? **That's the impact.**

The teacher who once resisted restorative practices but is now quick to organize a restorative circle?
That's transformation.

The student who now raises their hand with confidence.
That's legacy in motion.

Progress isn't always loud. But it is happening. As a leader, your job isn't just to push change forward. It's to recognize it when it happens and to name it. *To celebrate the moments when someone tries again, speaks up, shifts a habit, or extends grace.* Those moments, though small, are seeds. And with time, they grow into culture.

Leadership is as much about the pace of change as the change itself. Move too fast, and you risk leaving people behind. Move with care, and you build momentum that sticks.

So:

Celebrate the gains, even the small ones.

Honor the process, even when it's messy.

Stay the course, even when the road is slow.

Change isn't measured by how fast you go; it's measured

by how far you're willing to walk with others one step at a time.

The legacy you leave won't be built in one grand moment of change, but in the quiet, consistent ones that came before it.

Reflection Journal Starter

Change isn't always bold or fast; it's often quiet, layered, and rooted in relationships.

In a profession driven by urgency, it's tempting to equate movement with progress. But true transformation takes time and care. When we rush to fix, we often overlook the human side of change. When we lead with presence and persistence, we invite others into the process.

This legacy seed reminds us that sustainable leadership doesn't just name the need for change; it walks patiently alongside it. It values buy-in over compliance. And it recognizes that every courageous step (no matter how small) is worthy of celebration.

In connection with the earlier seeds, this reflection builds on the courage to leave your comfort zone and the willingness to release perfection. The journey toward equity and legacy isn't a race; it's a rhythm. Your job isn't to finish first, it's to help the community finish together.

Reflection Prompt:

Where have you seen signs of growth in your school that deserve celebration, even if they aren't fully complete?

How might naming and honoring those small wins build trust, momentum, and collective confidence?

Legacy Seed in Action:

Revisit one initiative, specifically name any signs of progress with your team. Celebrate these milestones as evidence that meaningful change takes time and remind your team that every step forward, no matter how small, matters.

Legacy Checkpoint:

Change that lasts is change that's cultivated. It grows from consistent steps, patient leadership, and a willingness to honor progress before perfection. Celebrate the unseen shifts. Uplift the quiet growth. Legacy lives in the moments that others might overlook.

Legacy Seed: Strong Schools Aren't Loud, They're Rooted

"The flash will fade. Build what lasts. Rooted leadership doesn't require volume."

– Legacy-Driven Leadership.

In school leadership, there's a subtle but dangerous myth:

That meaningful change must be loud.

That visibility equals value.

That performance is proven through spectacle.

But real transformation? It isn't flashy; it's foundational. It's not performative; it's principled. It's not theatrical. Just deeply rooted.

It's rarely about who's talking the loudest.

Strong schools aren't built on volume; they're built on alignment.

They are communities where adults operate with a shared compass, where students know what to expect, and where leadership is *felt* more than heard. The strength of a school is revealed not in the morning announcements or mission statement, but in how values are upheld when no one's watching.

It's not about the leader's spotlight.

It's not about the collective's root system.

In schools **rooted** in equity, care, and accountability, storms don't splinter culture. Leadership transitions don't unravel the community. Challenges don't undo years of progress. Why? Because their foundation is internal, nurtured by trust, aligned practices, and an unwavering belief in every student's worth.

My journey of confronting systems that promoted inequity wasn't loud. It was intentional.

It began within my school building, where we revisited policies, examined disproportional outcomes, and listened to student voices. But it didn't stop there. In my early years as a school administrator, I was invited to join a districtwide facilitation team, in collaboration with NYU, to lead sustained professional learning experiences focused on cultural responsiveness and equity. Together, we trained educators, administrators, secretaries, custodians, everyone who shapes the fabric of a school.

We explored topics that weren't always easy to name, such as white fragility, the myth of meritocracy, and systemic bias. Each training cycle brought new insights, resistance, and reflection. Some participants leaned in. Others pushed back. But we stayed rooted in the work.

We didn't lecture; we facilitated. We didn't demand agreement; we nurtured understanding and cultivated internal accountability.

And for me, the work wasn't theoretical. It was deeply personal. As a Black student who navigated inequitable systems in the south, and now as a Black educator working to transform them, I knew the stakes.

Every session, every courageous conversation, every seed we planted, it was about building the capacity in others to lead this work within their schools. Participants didn't just leave with knowledge, they left with a mandate: build equity teams, examine your systems, and root your leadership in justice, not just compliance.

That's what it means to lead from below the surface. Rooted leadership doesn't demand the spotlight; it builds systems that outlast it.

It's the courage to ask the hard questions long after the audience has left. It's the discipline to do the work even when no one applauds. It's the belief that the strongest schools aren't those with the loudest leaders, but those with the deepest roots.

Reflection Journal Starter

The most enduring schools don't rely on noise or performative gestures; they're anchored in values, relationships, and consistent, equity-centered action. Flash may catch attention, but foundation builds trust. This legacy seed calls us to examine what's truly shaping our school culture: Is it driven by the loudest voice, or by the values that hold firm when no one is watching?

Rooted leadership means investing in the work that doesn't always trend or garner praise, like cultivating cultural responsiveness, challenging the status quo, and empowering others to carry the work forward. Strong schools embed equity into their foundation, not just their rhetoric.

Reflection Prompt:

What values are most deeply rooted in your leadership, and how are you cultivating conditions where those values are lived, not just listed?

Legacy Seed in Action:

Spend 15 minutes in a high-functioning classroom, not to evaluate the teacher, but to notice how routines, relationships, and trust play a role beneath the surface. Afterwards, reflect on how these roots might inform the culture you're cultivating school-wide.

Legacy Checkpoint:

Loud leadership may grab attention, but rooted leadership builds a legacy. Your greatest impact won't be measured by how often you're seen—it will be revealed in how well your vision holds, even when you're no longer in the room.

Chapter Five Closing Reflection: Courage and Change

"When the dust of change settles, what remains is the legacy you've built; the roots you've planted, the values you've modeled, and the lives you've touched. Courageous leadership is not just about what you fight against, it's about what you're building toward."

– *Legacy-Driven Leadership*

Courage in school leadership doesn't always announce itself. Sometimes it whispers. Sometimes it shows up in quiet conviction, in the decision to try again, or in the willingness to stay at the table when the work gets hard. It's not about bravado; it's about cultivating psychological safety where people can feel free to speak their truth, make mistakes, and learn (Edmundson, 2019). Without this safety, change will stall.

In this chapter, we explored what it means to lead with courage, not as a momentary act, but as a way of being.

You began by **stepping outside the comfort zone**, not just your own, but the collective one. You examined the default settings that insulate schools from necessary change and leaned into the discomfort that true equity work requires.

You then **challenged the illusion of perfection**, choosing progress over performance. You embraced the idea that real leadership is grounded in presence, reflection, and learning out loud, not in getting everything right.

You paused to honor **the pace of real transformation**. You were reminded that going slow is not falling behind, it's leading in a way that lasts.

You were reminded that every small win is a signal: the work is working.

Finally, you **rooted yourself in values**. You let go of the need for visibility, trusting that leadership is measured not by how loud it is, but by how lasting. Each of these seeds builds upon the others: Courage disrupts. Growth humbles. Time refines. And depth sustains. This is the work of courageous leadership, not to manage change from a distance, but to meet it head-on with humanity, clarity, and resolve.

The most transformative leaders aren't always the loudest. They're the ones still standing when the noise fades, rooted, steady, and reaching forward.

When mistakes happen (as they always do), courage means owning the moment, replanting what we've pulled too soon, and remembering that we can choose wisdom over impulse. We don't have to trade flowers for weeds.

Chapter Six - Legacy and Purpose

Courage may move us forward, but it's purpose that gives the moment meaning. The changes made with courage become the legacies that we leave in care.

Legacy isn't built overnight; it's planted, nurtured, and cultivated over time through presence, decisions, and the people we empower along the way. True leadership is less about being remembered for a title and more about being remembered for your impact: on hearts, minds, and systems.

This chapter invites you to reflect on the mark you're leaving, not just in metrics or initiatives, but in the energy you bring, the culture you shape, and the values you model. Whether you lead as a "fountain" or a "drain", as a solitary figure or part of a creatively crazy cadre, you are always contributing to something greater than yourself.

Your greatest legacy may not be what you build. It may be how you *lead* while building it. The gift of leadership isn't found only in your actions; it's revealed in your presence.

Legacy Seeds in This Chapter:

- **Legacy Isn't Built Overnight** – *Legacy Takes Time*

- **Success Isn't Built, It's Planted** – *Every Decision is a Seed*

- **A Cadre of Creatively Crazy Individuals Can Carry an Organization** – *Cultivate the Creatively Crazy*

- **You Can Either Be a Fountain or a Drain** – *You Choose Which Way Water Flows*

- **The Greatest Gift Is Your Presence** – *Your Presence is a Present*

Legacy Seed: Legacy Isn't Built Overnight

"Legacy isn't built overnight; it's built every day, through presence, priorities, and purpose."

– *Legacy-Driven Leadership.*

Anyone can plant something…a punchy slogan, a program, a policy.

But legacy, the kind that lives beyond your leadership, isn't born in the moment you start something. It grows in what you stay with.

As mentioned in prior legacy seeds, the pressure to deliver quick wins is real. But fast decisions aren't always the right ones. And urgency without clarity can do more harm than good.

Legacy work is slower. Steadier. It's not driven by optics or politics; it's guided by intention.

In my leadership journey, I've seen what I now call the *initiative treadmill*: a nonstop rollout of programs and priorities, often launched in response to headlines or cultural waves. These efforts start with good intent, but without strong roots; without alignment to core values or structures, they fade. And when that cycle repeats, it wears down staff. It chips away at trust.

When people are asked to pivot again and again, without clarity or coherence, they don't just get tired. They lose faith.

Legacy isn't built through performance. It's built through

presence. It shows up in the patience to water what you've planted. In the discipline of pruning what no longer serves. In the courage to pause, reflect, and realign, not just react.

It's in the small decisions that no one sees:

Choosing consistency over novelty.

Saying "not yet" when a new initiative doesn't align.

Listening before launching.

Legacy-driven leadership is gardening work. The kind of work that requires you to protect the soil, to cultivate growth you may not even get to harvest during your tenure. But make no mistake, your impact is growing quietly, daily, and deeply.

What you build with intention will speak long after your name is no longer on the door.

Reflection Journal Starter:

Legacy isn't built in a rush; it's cultivated with care. In a profession that often rewards speed and short-term wins, choosing consistency and alignment is a radical act of leadership.

This seed reminds us that real change grows over time. It's deliberate. Rooted. Designed to outlast you and serve students long after you're gone.

Reflection Prompt:

Where in your leadership are you planting with intention, and how will students experience the difference between a moment of change and a culture that lasts?

Legacy Seed in Action:

Write down one legacy action you can take this month, no matter how small, and commit to it. To hold yourself accountable, share this action with a colleague. At the end of the month, reflect on the impact of this action and select your next step.

Legacy Checkpoint:

Legacy doesn't live in task lists or titles. It's found in the quiet discipline of leaders who tend to the soil, nurture growth, and stay the course. When you lead with vision and patience, you're not just building for today; you're preparing the ground for generations to come.

Legacy Seed: Success Isn't Built, It's Planted

"Success doesn't start with strategy; it starts with soil. What you plant today shapes what grows tomorrow."

-Legacy-Driven Leadership.

You can teach strategies. You can introduce walkthrough rubrics, design sharp systems, and lead data cycles with precision. But true success, the kind that transforms culture and shifts the trajectory of students' lives, isn't installed like a system. It's planted as a seed.

In school leadership, the impact you make isn't always visible in real time. Some changes occur quietly; through a shift in tone, in how a student starts to believe in themselves, or in when a teacher begins to see discipline as an opportunity for restoration, not control. These aren't the kinds of outcomes you can always track on a dashboard. They show up later in how a culture sustains itself or in how someone else begins to lead with care. That's how you know a seed took root.

Growth depends not just on the seed but also on the soil.

You'll only feel the faint confirmation when a former student circles back to tell you that your words mattered. When a colleague carries forward the vision you helped shape. When a system still holds long after you're gone.

Ask yourself:

What kind of soil are you tending?

Legacy-driven leaders cultivate conditions that allow others to thrive. They move beyond transactional leadership to a more transformative approach; one that centers values over urgency, alignment over optics, and people over compliance.

Legacy-driven leaders:

Plant confidence in students before correcting them.

Plant purpose in staff before demanding performance.

Plant dignity in systems before chasing results.

Like any seasoned gardener, legacy-driven leaders also:

Water what matters with visibility, encouragement, and consistency.

Weed out what hinders with the courage to remove bias, burnout, and bureaucracy.

Make room for new growth by dismantling outdated structures that marginalize the most vulnerable.

This specific seed is personal to me. I've witnessed the generational power of legacy-driven leadership. In one school, our unwavering commitment to equity slowly started to shift how Black boys were seen, disciplined, and supported. It didn't happen all at once. But I saw the shift begin. I saw roots form. And I knew that we had planted something that would grow. Legacy work involved planting seeds in soil that sustains all students. As Hernandez, Lopez, and Swier (2022) argue, dismantling disproportionality requires leaders to build systems that are culturally responsive and sustaining.

The baobab tree in the Kimoja Educational Consulting logo is more than a design. It's our blueprint. Its wide canopy and deep roots remind us that a real legacy isn't loud. It's quiet. Intentional. Rooted.

While you may never witness the full harvest, your leadership will live in every branch that grows from the values you plant.

Reflection Journal Starter

Success in schools doesn't grow from pressure or performance; it grows from daily acts of care, intention, and cultivation. As leaders, we're always planting seeds through the systems we build, the relationships we nurture, and the values we model. Some seeds will bloom quickly. Others may take years to show. But all of them matter.

Legacy isn't measured by the harvest; it's revealed in the soil you leave behind.

Reflection Prompt:

What seeds are you planting in your school today—and how will they shape the culture long after you've moved on?

Legacy Seed in Action:

Identify one relationship you can invest in this week that will strengthen your long-term impact. Take at least one intentional step that nurtures growth. This could be through offering support, scheduling time, or simply expressing appreciation.

Legacy Checkpoint:

Success isn't built through urgency; it's grown through purpose. When you lead with care, equity, and long-term vision, your legacy lives on—not in headlines or handbooks, but in people, practices, and possibilities.

Legacy Seed: A Cadre of Creatively Crazy Individuals Can Carry an Organization

"A cadre of creatively crazy, concerned individuals can carry an organization. But pockets of excellence don't create the hum of an excellent organization."

- Dr. Lorraine Monroe.

Every school has its bright spot - the magnetic teachers who connect effortlessly with every student, the paraprofessionals who turn obstacles into opportunities, the teaching assistants and counselors who make students feel seen, valued, safe, and capable. These are your "creatively crazy" change-makers; deeply invested, quietly brilliant, and always willing to go the extra mile.

I've always looked forward to stepping into their classrooms or spaces. The way they engaged students was equal parts magic and intention. They reminded me that great teaching is both an art and a discipline.

But pockets of brilliance aren't enough to transform a school.

One of my education heroes, Dr. Lorraine Monroe, once said,

"A cadre of creatively crazy, concerned individuals can carry an organization. But pockets of excellence don't create the hum an excellent organization has."

That quote has followed me to every school I've led. It doesn't just highlight a challenge; it offers a vision. A reminder that true transformation doesn't live in silos.

The hum, a concept that we explored earlier in this book,

isn't created by isolated excellence. It emerges when systems are aligned, when values are shared, and when the brilliance of the few becomes the blueprint for the many. It's the difference between scattered applause and organized harmony.

Legacy isn't built by the gifted few; it's built when their spark becomes embedded in the school culture. That means:

Moving from personality-driven excellence to system-supported excellence.

Shifting from hero educators to collaborative cultures.

Ensuring your brightest stars don't burn out but become beacons that guide others.

During my time as a middle school principal, I saw this firsthand. A handful of phenomenal educators became the heartbeat of the building. But over time, it became clear that their impact, while powerful, wasn't sustainable in isolation. The weight was heavy. And it wasn't equitable.

So, we shifted.

We created structures that turned leaders into catalysts.

Common planning time became a space for collective visioning. Instructional practices were aligned to school-wide goals. And we launched **The Marigold Project**, a peer-recognition initiative inspired by Jennifer Gonzalez's article *Find Your Marigold: The One Essential Rule for New Teachers*. In it, Gonzalez contrasts marigolds, plants that help others thrive, with walnut trees, which stunt growth. We invited our team to notice and name the "marigolds" among them; to elevate those who nurtured, supported, and inspired.
Slowly, the weight began to distribute. And the hum began to build.

In legacy-driven leadership, the goal isn't to find heroes. It's to cultivate ecosystems where excellence spreads, where the soil is rich enough for every seed to thrive.

Reflection Journal Starter:

Innovation rarely starts with a mandate. It often begins in the margins; within the classrooms of passionate, creatively crazy educators who imagine more for students. But brilliance without structure fades. Legacy-driven leaders treat these bright spots not as anomalies, but as seeds of transformation.

When we create the conditions for their brilliance to grow and spread, we begin to build a culture where excellence is no longer isolated. It's embedded.

Reflection Prompt:

How are you intentionally cultivating the conditions for your brightest faculty and staff members to thrive? How are you ensuring their impact reaches beyond their individual spaces?

Legacy Seed in Action:

Gather three creative colleagues for a 20-minute brainstorming session on a current challenge. Frame this time as an opportunity to generate bold, even "crazy" ideas that will support students and families without judgment. By creating intentional space for creative collaboration, without what could be considered traditional guardrails, you remind your team that innovation doesn't thrive in isolation. Innovation grows when a cadre of creatively crazy and passionate people think differently together.

Legacy Checkpoint:

Legacy lives not in moments of magic, but in the systems that multiply it. When you cultivate the hum by nurturing excellence, amplifying equity, and weaving collaboration into your school's fabric, you grow a culture that outlasts any one person. You plant shared power.

Legacy Seed: You Can Either Be a Fountain or A Drain

"*You can either be a fountain or a drain.*"

— *Ernie Johnson.*

I'm a huge basketball fan. One of my favorite voices in the game is Ernie Johnson—broadcaster, storyteller, and steady presence on TNT's *Inside the NBA*. Years ago, Johnson shared a simple reflection:

"You can either be a fountain or a drain."

That line stuck with me. I thought it was both clever and clarifying. It offered a mirror to every school leader, faculty member, and staff member. In schools, every hallway greeting, team meeting, and classroom walk-through carries emotional weight.

Here's the truth:

Leaders are emotional transmitters.

Whether intentionally or not, they either replenish the energy of those around them or deplete it.

And it's a choice.

You can choose to be a **fountain**:

Steady, present, and grounded.

Aware of your emotional landscape and intentional about how it affects others.

Someone who creates a sense of psychological safety, not one who leaves people bracing for the next reaction.

Or you can become a **drain**:

Reactive, inconsistent, unaware of how your stress leaks into the room.

Someone who might still achieve results on paper, but at the cost of trust, morale, and sustainability.

For me, presence has always been a leadership cornerstone, perhaps a byproduct of being a middle child. Long before I held formal titles, I paid attention to energy. I could feel the tension in a hallway interaction or the calm in a classroom conversation. That sensitivity became a consistent presence in my leadership journey.

When I began coaching other school leaders, I returned to the same truth:

Leadership isn't just about plans; it's about emotional presence. It's not only "What's the plan?" It's also, "What's the energy?"

Ultimately, your emotional tone sets the culture. It shapes how others show up, how they communicate, and how safe they feel doing the work. When leaders pause to reflect, especially under pressure, they notice how their presence either stabilizes or destabilizes the team.

Ask yourself daily:

Am I a fountain or a drain?

And maybe more importantly:

What am I pouring into my people?

Reflection Journal Starter:

Your leadership energy is contagious. Whether grounded or reactive, calm or chaotic, your emotional posture sets the tone for everyone around you.

Legacy-driven leadership doesn't require perfection. It calls for presence. It's not about suppressing your emotions; it's about owning them, processing them, and making sure your stress doesn't spill into the spaces your team relies on for stability.

When leaders lead like fountains, steady, restorative, and emotionally aware, they create the psychological safety others need to thrive, especially those most vulnerable to instability.

Reflection Prompt:

When pressure rises, how do you regulate your energy? What do others experience because of it?

Legacy Seed in Action:

At the end of your day, list three actions you took that added energy to your leadership team. Reflect on how those actions influenced the team's mood, momentum, and focus. Commit to repeating those actions tomorrow.

Legacy Checkpoint:

Leadership is a daily act of emotional stewardship. You will shape the climate whether you mean to or not. The only question is:

Will your presence nourish or drain?

Legacy Seed: The Greatest Gift is Your Presence

"Presence is the most powerful gift a leader can offer. It tells your people: You matter. I'm here. Let's build together."

– Legacy-Driven Leadership.

You've already seen how presence shapes trust, connection, and school culture. But here, at the edge of your legacy, presence becomes something more: it becomes your **lasting imprint**.

In school leadership, presence isn't passive; it's powerful.

It's not just about being seen; it's about being **felt**. The kind of leadership that is mentally engaged, emotionally grounded, and fully attuned to the people around you.

This is grounded leadership. Steady. Human, Purposeful.

It sets the tone. It anchors the culture. It communicates care in ways no strategy, slogan, or spreadsheet ever could.

Yes, the paperwork matters and deadlines exist. But leadership is formed through the moments that matter, not just the tasks that accumulate.

These moments don't require a title. They don't need a script. But they *do* require you.

A smile at arrival that eases a child's anxiety.

A quick hallway check-in that reminds a staff member

they're not alone.

A moment of quiet recognition when someone needs to feel seen.

These aren't distractions from leadership; they're the roots of it.

Throughout my career, I've witnessed the quiet power of leaders who stay grounded, especially in those moments of immense pressure. I've coached others to do the same.

When you lead with intention instead of impulse, and relationship instead of reaction, you begin to understand that the most powerful leadership isn't reactive, it's relational.

It doesn't mean being everywhere. But it does mean that wherever you are, you are fully there.

When leaders commit to being attuned, emotionally, relationally, and culturally, they shift the experience for everyone:

Students feel safer.

Staff feel steady.

Families feel like partners, not bystanders.

Legacy-driven leadership means showing up with your full self, especially when it's inconvenient, quiet, or unseen. Not to prove yourself, but to **anchor others**.

Legacy doesn't echo from a distance. **It takes root where you stand.**

Reflection Journal Starter:

True presence in leadership isn't about being everywhere; it's about being fully there when it counts. It's about the moments when your quiet consistency becomes someone else's stability, when your unseen gestures of care lay the groundwork for trust. Presence is how you honor humanity in a system that often forgets it. And over time, it becomes a rhythm; one that shapes how people feel, function, and flourish under your leadership.

Legacy-driven leadership means showing up not just to manage, but to ground, connect, and heal.

Reflection Prompt:

When you enter a space, physically or emotionally, what do people feel?

How does your presence restore, reassure, or re-center those who need it most?

Legacy Seed in Action:

Spend 10 minutes today giving undivided attention to someone who often gets overlooked – a student, staff member, or colleague. Listen fully without distractions. These small moments of presence leave the deepest mark.

Legacy Checkpoint:

Your presence is more than a leadership trait; it's a **living imprint**.

It communicates what you value, how you lead, and who belongs. When you show up with intentionality and care, your leadership extends beyond plans and policies—it roots itself in people.

And long after the meetings are over, your presence will remain - in the culture you helped grow, and in the people you chose to truly see.

Chapter Six Closing Reflection: Legacy & Purpose

"Your legacy is written in the soil; in the seeds you plant when no one is watching."

– Legacy-Driven Leadership.

Legacy isn't measured in noise, notoriety, or name recognition.

It's measured in the systems you strengthen, the culture you nurture, and the people you empower. Whether you realize it or not, you are always planting something.

This chapter reminded us that legacy doesn't live in slogans or surface-level wins. It's not fast. It's not flashy. It's not performative.

Legacy is built through quiet, repeated, intentional choices, especially when no one is watching. Each time you lead with clarity, care, and consistency, you deepen the roots of your impact.

We redefined success, not as an outcome to chase, but as a seed to plant. And planting takes patience. It means investing in others, knowing you may never see the harvest. But when your work is rooted in purpose, the impact lives on.

As Dr. Lorraine Monroe said:

"A cadre of creatively crazy individuals can carry an organization."

True excellence doesn't rely on isolated brilliance. It

hums when your values echo in every classroom, and when the spark of a few becomes the culture of the whole.

Legacy-driven leadership is never about the spotlight.

It's about the soil you leave behind.

Epilogue: The Seeds We Leave Behind

"You don't harvest on the same day you plant. Legacy takes time to root, grow, and bear fruit."

– *Legacy-Driven Leadership.*

Legacy isn't a title. It's not defined by a single year, a standout initiative, or even a flawless run. It's a slow, rooted unfolding, one decision, one conversation, one brave act at a time.

Throughout this book, we've explored a different kind of leadership:

A legacy-driven one.

A people-centered one.

One that lives beyond compliance and policy, and takes root in presence, purpose, and equity.

We've unpacked six core chapters, each offering a seed for reflection and a blueprint for action:

- **Vision & Intention** - grounded in clarity and purpose.

- **Trust** - as the foundation for culture and communication.

- **Presence** - which centers people over paperwork.

- **Growth -** that begins with self-reflection, not

mandates.

- **Courage** - to challenge the status quo and move at the pace of impact.

- **Legacy & Purpose** - reminding us we are planters, not just performers.

This isn't easy work. But it's sacred work. The kind of work that matters long after the metrics fade.

If you've made it to this point, it's because you already are what this book affirms:

A cultivator. A builder. A possibility-maker. A gardener.

So here is your invitation:

Keep planting with intention.

Keep leading with clarity.

Keep showing up, especially when it's inconvenient.

Keep being the kind of leader whose presence builds safety, whose decisions build culture, and whose values build a legacy that lives beyond your role.

Your title may change. Your school may shift. But the roots you plant, in people, in systems, in community, will remain.

Thank you for holding space with me inside these pages. May the seeds you plant today bloom into something lasting, something worthy of your calling. Use your wisdom to discern when you've pulled flowers to make room for weeds so that you can own up to it and pivot.

If you're ready to keep growing, turn to the **Legacy-Driven Leadership Reflective Journal** and **Facilitator's Guide**. Whether you're planting alone or with a team, these tools will help you deepen your practice, revisit your purpose, and continue building a legacy that lasts.

Closing Reflection: What a Seed Can Do…

Legacy is what a seed can do when the soil remembers.

– Legacy-Driven Leadership.

This image of a seed breaking through stone as it grows into a baobab tree, and the quote that anchors it, holds three truths.

On one level, it's about **growth**; how something small can become something strong when the conditions are right.

It's also about **leadership**; the kind that roots new ideas in the wisdom of what came before.

Deeper still, it's about **memory**; the kind that carries us, the kind that whispers of the ancestors whose blood and labor enriched the ground we now stand on.

When the soil remembers, it doesn't just nourish the seed; it honors the story that made its growth possible.

A seed is small, often unnoticed, but it carries a quiet defiance. Planted in the right place, and sometimes even in the hardest places, it finds a way to grow. It doesn't rush. It doesn't demand permission. It simply roots, pushes, and expands until the world around it makes room. Leadership is much the same. The work you've begun, the conversations you've sparked, the people you've poured into, these are seeds. They may not break the surface in your time, but they will find their moment.

Sometimes those seeds do more than move obstacles; they split them wide open. In your leadership, you will meet stone: resistance, weight, and walls. What you plant with intention, courage, and care can transform those barriers into gateways.

The seeds you've encountered in these pages are only a few among many. Some you will discover in your journey, uniquely shaped by your experiences, challenges, and communities.

As I wrote in the epilogue, your legacy is not in the noise you make, but in the lives you change. Trust that what you've planted will grow; sometimes in ways you'll never see, but always in ways that matter. Your impact isn't what defines you; it's the thing that helps define who's behind you.

I realized how often the word *performance* appeared in my writing as I reached the end of this book. At first, I considered addressing the frequency through revision. But then I stopped to wonder: **why did it show up so often**? I realized there might be a reason. That frequency says something. It reflects the tension that I've felt in my own leadership journey; the pull to perform versus the responsibility to build something lasting.

If there is one lesson I hope echoes beyond these pages,

it is this: performance may earn applause, but that applause can be deceptive. It often comes from those satisfied with the show, rather than committed to the substance. Whether knowingly or unknowingly, that applause sustains the very cycles of stagnation that keep schools from growing. Legacy, by contrast, rarely earns the loudest applause in the moment; it plants the trust that makes lasting change possible.

Legacy is what a seed can do when the soil remembers.

Acknowledgments

This book would not exist without the seeds planted in me by others: family, mentors, colleagues, and students; those who shaped the way I lead, learn, and live.

To my family - thank you for being the roots. To my mother, whose passion for young people spilled into me, my stepfather, who stepped up to be my dad, and to my brothers and sisters; thank you for believing in me.

To my wife Tashawna: your love, your grounding presence, and your unwavering belief in me have held me steady through every season of growth. To my children, you are my legacy. What I dream, craft, and build is ultimately for you. Use the seeds planted to be disruptive. You are your ancestors' wildest dreams.

To the educators and co-conspirators that I've worked alongside over the years, thank you for your dedication, your trust, and your commitment to equity, even when it's hard. The stories in this book were shaped in real hallways, in real classrooms, during real challenges, and it's your presence that gave them life. To Jasmine Brown, who helped craft my leadership blueprint, and to Derek Johnson, who stood in the trenches with me for years, thank you. For school leaders like Ken Mayfield and Millie Torres, I made this book with you in mind.

To the faculty and staff of the schools I've led: your courage to grow, reflect, and challenge the status quo inspired these pages. You are more than colleagues; you are co-authors in the legacy we built together. We were in the trenches together, and we celebrate the fruits of our collective labor together.

I would like to personally thank two amazing educators that I've come to know as family: Jacquie Johnson ("Cuz") and Louise Gundrum. Thank you both for walking with me during my leadership journey. Cuz, you were and are still my sounding board. Your words of encouragement served as fuel for me during my first few years as an administrator; I appreciate you dearly, bredren. Louise, you supported me during my transition into principalship and became a trusted confidant in the trenches. Without your guidance and confidence in my vision, we would not have been able to accomplish what we did as a leadership team.

To the countless students who've allowed me to lead and learn from them: your voices, your resilience, and your brilliance are why this work matters. You are the center of it all. There is a special handful of you that are especially close to my heart, and I appreciate you. I hope I continue to inspire the legacy that you're crafting.

To my mentors and leadership coaches: thank you for

showing me what it looks like to lead with both strength and humanity. Your wisdom echoes throughout this book.

Finally, to the reader: thank you for showing up. For your courage to reflect. For your willingness to lead with legacy in mind. May these seeds grow something powerful in your leadership journey and in the lives you impact. This book intentionally ends with **The Blueprint to Legacy-Driven Leadership**. Let it challenge you, affirm you, and remind you that the most powerful legacies are planted with intention and tended with humility.

As you read each line of the blueprint, ask yourself:

Where am I already living this?

Where do I need to grow?

What kind of leadership will I leave behind?

With deep gratitude,

Jason Rogers
Founder, Kimoja Educational Consulting
Co-Founder, The Kimoja Initiative

The Blueprint to Legacy-Driven Leadership

A parting gift...

The Blueprint to Legacy-Driven Leadership

A framework to return to as your journey unfolds.

This blueprint is not a formula to follow perfectly. It's a framework to reflect on, adapt, and return to over time. *Let it challenge you, affirm you, and remind you that the most powerful legacies are planted with intention, nurtured through consistency, and tended with humility.*

Vision & Intention

- See the future before you build it.
- Catch the vision and hold it tight.
- Name your gift and why it matters.
- Plant seeds, not just plans.
- Let purpose guide every step.

Trust as the Foundation for Leadership

- Build trust before structures.
- Position others to take your spot.
- Honor your word in small and large things.

- Welcome others into the vision.
- Ask for help and offer it freely.

The Presence Principle

- Be visible, even when it's hard.
- Listen deeper than words.
- Align your actions with your values.
- Let people feel your care daily.
- Be consistent in all spaces and with all faces.

Growth & Accountability

- Confront what you've allowed.
- Lead with courage through conflict.
- Reflect, recalibrate, and rise again.
- Own the outcome, not just the effort.
- Celebrate growth and name the gaps.

Courage & Change

- Intentionally step out of your comfort zone

- Face the fears that hold culture back
- Protect equity even when challenged.
- Demonstrate wisdom over impulse.
- Reimagine systems to serve all.

Legacy & Purpose

- Lead beyond your tenure.
- Build teams that outlast you.
- Share your wisdom generously.
- Respect the journey and those who walk it with you.
- Protect what matters most.

References and Recommended Reading

These works informed the ideas in *Legacy-Driven Leadership* and offer valuable resources for leaders who want to go deeper into trust, culture, equity, and legacy-driven leadership.

- Bukko, D. (2021). *Building trust in schools: Strategies from high-trust principals. Planning and Changing, 50*(1–2), 1–22.
- Edmondson, A. (2019). *The fearless organization: Creating psychological safety in the workplace for learning, innovation, and growth.* Wiley.
- Hernández, M. G., López, D., & Swier, R. (2022). *Dismantling disproportionality: A culturally responsive and sustaining systems approach.* Teachers College Press.
- Hong, J. Y. (2020). Teachers' trust in principals and their well-being during school transitions. *Frontiers in Education, 5,* 108. https://doi.org/10.3389/feduc.2020.00108
- Jack, J. B. (2023). Principal visibility and teacher trust: Impacts on teacher morale and engagement. *Journal of School Administration Research and Development, 8*(1), 14–26.

- Leithwood, K., Louis, K. S., Anderson, S., & Wahlstrom, K. (2023). *How leadership influences student learning: Updated edition*. The Wallace Foundation.
- Lisi, D., & Friesen, S. (2025). Leadership practices of middle school principals that promote collective teacher efficacy. *Canadian Journal of Educational Administration and Policy, 2025*(199), 1–25.
- National Equity Project. (2020). *Leading for equity: The pursuit of excellence in education*. National Equity Project. https://www.nationalequityproject.org
- McIntosh, P. (1988). *White privilege and male privilege: A personal account of coming to see correspondences through work in women's studies* (Working Paper No. 189). Wellesley College Center for Research on Women.

www.ingramcontent.com/pod-product-compliance
Lightning Source LLC
Chambersburg PA
CBHW050107170426
43198CB00014B/2487